The Belinda Blinked Character Rankings
#122 to #1

By Rocky Flintstone
& Sammy Yeo;

Foreword by Cian O'Mahony

Rocky Flintstone;

Welcome to this wonderful source of knowledge on the Belinda Blinked universe. If you've gotten this far, then it goes without saying that you probably know who Rocky Flintstone is... yes, it's me.
What you may not know is who my co-author Sammy Yeo is. Well let me fill you in, in the nicest way possible. Sammy is Australian and lives in Melbourne. He's never really told me what he does, but he's definitely associated with the stage and arts and has a good education. I say this with confidence as he had very few spelling mistakes in his writing. Perhaps he uses spell checker?
I hear you saying to yourself, thanks for nothing Rocky... but how did these character rankings get written?
Good question and here is what I've been told by Sammy himself.

When the pandemic hit Australia, everything literally closed down overnight... much like the rest of the world. But Australia was slightly different in that you couldn't even leave your state of residence. So, Sammy found himself stuck in Melbourne and decided to relieve his boredom by ranking every character who'd appeared in the Belinda Blinked books. This took him some time, because not only did he rank them, he told us why he'd done so... for each character. This turned out to be a major undertaking and when he finally published his scorings, he sent me a copy. Thank you, Sammy!
I had a quick read through and to be honest I was impressed and also thought it deserved a wider audience. I also asked him to include the characters found in Lockdown 69... my small contribution, just like Sammy's, to the ongoing pandemic. We then included the Xmas specials and here we are. Well not quite, because I decided I would reply to every one of Sammy's comments and not just a one line reply, but a bit of in depth analysis and some more back story on various characters. Enough said, I hope you get as much enjoyment from reading this as we both did in writing it.

Rocky Flintstone
Summer 2022

Foreword by Cian O'Mahony

London, 15:32 BST, local time.

Cian Blinked; it wasn't a dream. Writer extraordinaire and legendary recluse Rocky Flintstone had just emailed him once again. "What is it this time?" he wondered in the dead London heat, brushing aside some crumbs from a Tit-Tat Crunchy. Rocky had emailed many times before, but this time was different. An attachment? 40,000 words? A NEW BOOK? A bead of sweat snaked its way down his forehead as he clicked the attachment. "My giddy Norses!" he exclaimed. The attachment contained a treasure trove of information any Belinda Blinked fan could desire. Not just desire, need. "This is the high life!" Cian thought as the ornate coat stand in the corner fell to the ground for no reason in particular. He cried into the night "This is heaven on a hat stand! Certainly not a pup or the office cat! This book is as high class as an evening at the Ritz and would fetch a high price at the next charity tombola!". With that, he poured another gin and tonic directly down his Patagonia t-shirt, started reading the book and settled in for a wild ride.

Now that that's out of the way I am Cian! You might remember me (or more likely not at all) from the podcast footnotes episode (Season 6, footnotes 3) when I went though my Belinda Blinked timeline (*cough* belindablumenthal.business *cough*) with Jamie, James and Alice. I also moderate the official My Dad Wrote A Porno subreddit with Rocky himself (reddit.com/r/MyDadWroteaPorno).

One of the true pleasures of making my timeline website was not just being able to be a guest on the podcast but to chat to Rocky from time to time. He is an absolutely lovely man and is great to his fans. Recently he shared an advance copy of his new book "The

Belinda Blinked Character Rankings" with me, which he co-wrote with the lovely Sammy Yeo. I'm just here to tell you that this book is well worth a read, in fact, it is a must read for the Belinda enthusiast.

I know you're eager to get stuck into this book so I won't keep you much longer but it is a fascinating read. Sammy will take you through the list of the best characters and Rocky will provide sassy remarks, character inspirations and backstory along with some all new content. The new scenes uncovered in this book will rock the fandom for sure. The scenes are hilarious and shed so much light on the story that you could fill another two podcast series on it. You will even get a sneak peak into where the plot might indeed be going. Then again maybe not. Exciting times are ahead for you!

So enjoy this book dear reader.
As Belinda herself would say,
"when you get what you want, you feel great!".

Cian O'Mahony.
August 2022,
London.

Contents;

The Top 100;
Chi-Chi the Parrot;
Dick Van Dyke;
The Other Executive(s);
Giselle's sex-starved Dutch-slash-Belgian mother;
Ethel;
Thick-rimmed glasses (Edmund) and his colleague ("Lunchbreaks");
Norman Asquith OBE;
Doc Al;
Bobby Blumenthal;
Footman at Harold's of London;
Geoffrey Drabble and Henry Babble;
The Ranch Crew (Chuck and Doug);
Miguel the waiter;
Dave Wilcox;
Cornelius Kettle;
The service station attendant;
The Hunts Girls;
Benny, Bella's brother;
Mrs Huddlesbird;
Jim Walters;
Quince;
Hazel the [co-] pilot;
Norm from next door;
Sydney the PA;
The BB3 commentators;

The Top 75;
Natasha Biles and Samantha Jones;
The McDonagh brothers;
Dr Veronica Studd;
The Bothy Man;
Chantelle;
Mr Hushman;
Monty Jim the Pizza Boy;
Jim Thompson;
Madeleine Chocolat;
Andy Milston;
Fanny Driller;
Digby Dodd;
The Belgian Butler;
Aldo Fellini;
Peggie Strumpethouse;
Gloria Ridley;
The Minister;
Betty Wilks and Vic Woods;
Adaam;
Monty, the Anciently House Master of the Keys;
Zachariah;
Claus Bloch;
The Prime Minister;
Patrick "Paddy" O'Hamlin;
Norman Togui;

The Top 50;
God;
Cedric;
Paddy the Barman;
James Dribble;
Tony Sylvester;
Mimi;
Señor Zip;
Ken Dewsbury;
Grigor Calanski;
Contessa Luccia Lorenzo;
Clarence, Duke of Epsom;
Cristina Rouse;
Alfonse Stirbacker;
Ian Snail;
Hans and Greta Schweinsteiger;
D'Artagnan Raspberry;
Aunty Bobbi, Uncle Ariel, and their baby rottweiler Fizzfudge;
Bill from HR;
Countess Zara of Leningrad;
Old Mother Blumenthal;
Peter Rouse;
Cosmo Macaroon;
Professor Slinz;
Chiara Montague;
Petra;

Introduction by Sammy Yeo who had the inspiration to produce these rankings...;

The world of *Belinda Blinked* has seen me through some rough moments:
Breakups;
Interminable covid lockdowns...
You name it...
The profound, erotic, and hysterical novels which sit at the heart of the *My Dad Wrote a Porno* podcast are never predictable and always surprising. What begins as a series of woefully mundane sexual encounters becomes a broad canvas on a Dickensian scale, as author Rocky Flintstone shifts genres, styles, and occasionally tenses, and leaves the reader spellbound. It's a world populated by wondrous, individual, and downright bizarre figures, from the ski slopes of Scotland and the seedy underworld of Amsterdam to downtown Texas and the Australian outback.

Naturally, this book contains extensive spoilers for every chapter up until the end of book six, including the yearly Christmas specials from 2016 until 2021 and the written special *Lockdown 69.* It includes every character with a speaking role, and a few besides. All of them brought to life by Rocky's magical pen and the chameleon-like vocal talents of his traumatised son... Jamie Morton.

Before we begin, I should offer a shout-out to those figures in group scenes who didn't make the rankings by virtue of being background extras only...
The wives and girlfriends at the tombola;
The sloppily-dressed women on Belinda's themed flight;
The twenty thousand ladies who are now proud owners of a non-stick tin wok;
Alfonse's fellow library members;
The Belgian press corps;
The dirty TGWU lorry drivers behind that glass screen;
All those wedding guests... (hi to the skillet table!);
The well-sated patrons of the Moulin Marron;
The many paramedics and neuroscientists who saved our beloved Bella;
Some oversexed Australian backpackers;

Bisch's caterers;
The sceptical crowds at the Pots and Pan Pacific Cookware Conference;
The nude denizens of heaven;
and everyone at Steele's Pots and Pans...
except Trevor fucking Ditherhead.

Not ranked: An altar boy.
This kid did a fantastic job in admitting Belinda to that church up in Scotland but I cannot sully this pure soul by including him on such a salacious list.

Rocky's Comment;
No comment… I've always wanted to say this, and now seems like the perfect opportunity… for once… and once only.

.

122. Katrina Pollet;

"Katrina Pollet is total shit…" James Cooper.
Last seen at the Battwood Park Under 19 Ladies Show Jumping Trials
Event and hopefully never seen again. A disgrace to the Pollet-Montague
dynasty. There are no best effort prizes here, sweetheart.

Rocky's Comment;
Most people totally misunderstand Katrina, she's there doing her thing…
and we all know if you don't do… you don't succeed. Besides practice
makes perfect, if you don't get into the kitchen, you'll never break an egg.
So come on Katrina… get your finger out and keep trying just like your
mama!!

121. Buster Broomfinger;

Technically he only appears as a noise offscreen. And technically he doesn't exist, at least in our timeline. But this jealous, petty little man had a huge impact on his wife Gertrude's life. Where Jane Austen's characters' level of morality can be detected by how willing they are to follow society's rules, and Ian McEwan's figures reveal their ethical compass through symbolism and atmosphere, Rocky takes a different approach: ask yourself how willing is this character to rip off their clothes, fold them neatly into a corner, and then spread something wide. If the answer is "very", chances are they're redeemable. Buster Broomfinger, by contrast, lives a horrid, sexless life. He exists as the series' greatest lesson in how never, *ever* to behave if you're in a relationship.

Rocky's comment;
Buster is the typical bully, someone never to get romantically involved with, you've been warned. To be honest, the real message I wanted to convey through Busters short appearance is really all about Gertrude. "One moment you're cock of the dung heap and the next a feather duster…" Jamie Morton.
How far are the mighty fallen… one click of the Norse Gods fingers and you go from the head of MI6, A Duchess with serious Royalty contacts to a battered wife in a bad relationship… be careful, it could be any of us…

120. The Grosvenor manservant;

Why is this guy taking orders from Claus Bloch? Why didn't he intervene when theriomorphic howls bellowed from the non-smoking section of the restaurant? How does he hold down a relationship when he comes home from work each day stinking of blue cheese fish mousse? *Nil points.*

Rocky's Comment;
I actually wrote this scene with Claus and Belinda pictured in a private suite, well that was my intention. I was also pretty pleased when this guy had the experience not to intervene... someone was having a very good time and if there was no blood seeping under the door... well, they're both adults.

119. The Tall Blonde Man (Amsterdam);

This guy just counts people. To be fair, they're people in a shop window orgy, but you've gotta work harder to climb these rankings, mate.

Rocky's Comment;
This guy is a professional heavy… he keeps the front door and listens out for passwords such as "My Auntie is Sick" He's also around if anyone decides to cause any trouble and the girls upstairs love him as he always sees them personally into their cab at any hour of the night. So, Sammy do me and you a favour … don't upset this guy too much…

118. Monsieur Rideaux;

Minister for Trade of the Belgian Colonies. His performance at the Reading Room orgy was underwhelming, if we're being honest (his four minutes expired without... you know), and his job title is questionable in light of established history. Although we must be impressed that Monsieur Rideaux managed to carry his business cards around while bone-naked.

Rocky's Comment;
I was hoping some bright spark would translate this very French name into English... Rideaux means curtains which in English slang means the end, kaput. No doubt if his masters had caught him in this situation it would have been curtains for his political career. Still, he's a good operator and at the time of writing similar officials were being caught with their pants, and more, down around their ankles in similar circumstances. Obviously in the Belgian Colonies, what goes around, comes around. The business cards are very easy to explain... he clenched them in the crack at the top of his ass... simple?

117. The Ritz Spa attendant;

Let's give credit to this attendant for getting a job at the most popular (and possibly only) venue in London. And she was able to spout a full, uninterrupted monologue about the packages on offer at the day spa. Then again, when you're in conversation with Belinda and Giselle, interruptions are fairly infrequent…

Rocky's Comment;
Lovely lady, very attractive and attentive but knows when to keep a secret… I wink my eye.
Of course, the Ritz in London is a very upmarket place and totally not where you'd find Belinda and Giselle normally hanging out. It's the juxtaposition of trash and posh that I so love about this scene… not that I'm alluding to any Steeles Pots and Pans employees being trashy… where's Bella???

116. Francesca;

This hotel receptionist in the South Sea Islands got more than she bargained for in *Lockdown 69* when she took the exquisitely-named D'Artagnan Raspberry home for the night. She's a classic Bond girl but chose to sleep with the baddie, and for that she cannot be rewarded.

Rocky's Comment;
I totally disagree, Francesca was duped by Raspberry and we can only hope she learnt from her hard earned experience. Totally ravishing, with skin to die for, this girl will go far. So much so that when we're filming this scene on location, I fully intend to look her up... and buy her a gin and tonic. Can't wait! Sammy, do you have the name of the hotel where she worked... jus askin...

115. Colonel Reginald Anthony George Sylvester;

Tony's dad has a minimal presence in the *Belinda Blinked* books, but is instantly recognisable due to his brusque moustache and obviously widowed demeanour. As the man who sired the despicable George, Colonel Sylvester might be considered unintentionally to blame. Given the books take place over a matter of weeks, it's been a rollercoaster ride for him:

son gets engaged;

the family plan and execute a wedding in a matter of days;

second son returns from the dead;

daughter-in-law betrays the family and flees to the continent;

second son turns out to be a traitor;

first son gets a new Irish lover;

daughter-in-law comes crawling back;

second son suffers a mishap... as experts often refer to a bloody death.

Lucky that Tony has that new job to pay for his dad's therapy...

Rocky's Comment;

Yes... "rollercoaster ride" is an astute observation... but first I want to state the obvious... no one has picked this up much to my chagrin... look at the man's initials for the Norse God's sake... RAGS... do you get it?

Yes, his nerves will indeed be torn to rags by the end of his life through his younger son's depravity and his older son's inability to pick a suitable wife. Whoops... maybe that's not a so uncommon feature of army life?

But yes, RAGS is a character in a family that truly deserves a back story.

114. Cricklewood Fisherman;

The podcast team were unable to resolve whether it's appropriate to shag in a reservoir but this oldish man has made his decision. And he's not afraid to chase young lovers through the reeds to make his point. Mind your own business, old timer!

Rocky's Comment;
As a past fly fisherman myself I fully endorse the sentiments of this denizen of the reservoir. One of my favourite memories is fly fishing in a local reservoir in late August on a glorious South Armagh evening as big moths began to hatch and fly over the water. The fish began to rise... which means they jump out of the water, to eat the moths as they landed heavily on the surface. The skill of putting a large piece of twisted feather and hook in the right place at the right time meant you went home with tomorrow's evening meal... and fish is good for you! The sad thing of course was we didn't have a Cricklewood tower for any young frisky people to hide in.

113. Lara Alexandra Kuznetsov;

Grigor's right-hand woman. She's probably pretty sexy (Jamie hopes she's based on Lara Croft) but Lara's xenophobia against the English is deeply unpleasant (if accurate, in this instance). Lara was last seen disappearing into the night with Peter Rouse, so by now she's probably covered in symbols and mentally enslaved to him. It might be for the best.

Rocky's Comment;
I have big plans for Lara... the problem is no one likes her boss Grigor Calanski... However, the world of Belinda Blinked moves on at a frightening speed. Perhaps we'll see a power struggle at the top of Grigor's empire when he eventually succumbs to the inevitable tycoon heart attack brought on by the increasing price of caviar. Let's wait and see...

112. Gladys;

The Steele's Pots and Pans' dinner lady; Gladys appears to have been mysteriously replaced by Ethel in recent years (see below). If Rocky's forgotten her, so will I.

Rocky's Comment;
Gladys will always live on in my heart... she was a dear soul, ridden with arthritis, but every day you could rely on that tea cart being painfully pushed to your open office door. A mug of strong, hot tea would be dispensed from the highly polished urn and you'd reach into your desk drawer for a chocolate digestive biscuit... paradise. Have a happy retirement Gladys, you fully deserve it.

<u>111. The Dutch taxi driver;</u>

Zipping between Schiphol airport and Rouse Supermarkets' head office, this taxi driver seemed to know a lot about Belinda's calendar. Could he be an undercover ally of Agent Helga? (Or could he have *been* Helga? She's a master of disguise, after all...)

Rocky's Comment;
No, this is just a jobbing taxi driver who's got a bit of an angle going with Cristina Rouse. Cristina needs people like taxi drivers to keep the cogs turning at her husband's supermarket empire and with people like Dr Robbins to look after, she needs all the help she can get. Another great contact is the lift repair man... he's at the offices most days fixing the antique lift and ingratiating himself... like the taxi driver, with Cristina. These guys know which side their ass is buttered on... but the question is, does Peter?

110. Kristian Crisotosis;

The owner of a South Sea Island speedboat, Kristian didn't get any sexual action in *Lockdown 69*. However, he did prove to be on the side of the angels by reporting a shady boat passenger, and thus saving Steele's from one of the most dramatic heists in kitchenware history. And he's now several thousand USD dollars richer, so everyone wins.

Rocky's Comment;
Kristian, while not a multimillionaire has the job everyone wants. Beautiful surroundings, great climate, owns a fast and sexy speed boat running a taxi service between the local islands. No doubt he takes his girlfriend fishing at the weekend as he's the sort of guy who knows how to give a girl a good time. Yes Kristian, I envy you your lifestyle... and pass the white wine!

109. The Tall Man (Tombola);

Responsible for hosting the charity shagfest in honour of the Asses and Donkeys Trust (remember them?), this guy is also capable of a good, dry joke once in a while. He seems to have deliberately rigged the tombola so that the Duchess would end up with Belinda, so perhaps he is actually MI6 himself. Can he be found operating the deep-fat fryer at It Curry Be Wurst? Either way, it is my dream that when Rocky (God forbid) wraps up the series, we get a return trip to the very important annual charity event.

Rocky's Comment;
To me the Tall Man is someone who could easily be expanded into a short story... he has sooo much potential character and mystique around him. How does he know Sir James, why does he organise the Tombola, why is he tall? All questions I know I should answer some day soon. Perhaps he's the local plumber... who knows, but I suspect Belinda likes him and he likes Belinda...

108. Samantha;

Sales assistant at Forster's of Knightsbridge. She doesn't seem especially efficient, but you have to respect her discretion and commitment to a most unusual workplace. Given that Forster's clearly has no upper age limit for its staff, Samantha can look forward to a long career providing jodhpurs to the many skinny women the Duchess hustles through its doors.

Rocky's Comment;
I love the name Samantha... so sexy and sophisticated... way better than Belinda...
As a sales assistant Samantha is the epitomy of discretion, soft talking, unfazed and totally loyal to Cedric. Perhaps she's a relative. These sort of, older established businesses do tend to recruit from within the family. Whatever, she's a great example of a modern day sales assistant and where would we all be without them? Anyone fancy another glass of Champers?

107. Artie Ridley;

Look, I know dads are dads, but don't go calling our heroine Melinda, ya feel me?

Rocky's Comment;
Sammy is right... don't insult our Belinda... do ya understand?
Artie is a knobhead of course, one of those typical London characters who think they know everything whilst actually knowing nothing and boasting about it! May well make a return to the pages of Belinda Blinked sometime never! The fact he runs a pub and is Bella's dad, does however give him a chance of future recompense.

106. Tara Gold;

TV executive-cum-journalist (however that works), Tara Gold never fulfilled her promise after we first met her as an exclusive guest of the Duke and Duchess of Epsom. If she spent less time enjoying the *haute cuisine* of the aristocracy... defrosted chicken kiev *and* trifle? what grandeur!... perhaps she'd find herself a story.

Rocky's Comment;

Tara Gold is the one character who got away from the series. I don't really know why it happened, but she's basically been eclipsed by Chiara Montague who was also at that infamous dinner party. Perhaps when Belinda needs a PR type person Tara could come into her own... let's wait and find out.

105. Sammy Quinn;

What a jerk. The former accounting manager of Steele's, Sammy was the least impressive figure in *Lockdown 69*, mounting an operation to launder millions from the company, only to find himself on the wrong end of a gun. I can understand why a Steele's accountant might be disillusioned, seeing so much money going toward massive giveaways and expensive space-age tables, but this is the wrong way to go about it, Quinn. You're trash, and I'm ashamed to share a name with you.

Rocky's Comment;
In real life, I was lucky enough to go to school with Sammy Quinn. Armagh City was a small place even back then, but Sammy and I did love our visits to the first Planetarium built in the British Isles. That was why I was amazed when I heard several years later that he'd become an accountant. It didn't make any sense. You see Sammy couldn't do maths to save his own life...
By the way for future potential actors, his accent is best read in pure "Norn Iron" speak... that's Northern Ireland English to you guys.

104. Virgil;

The pilot for Jim Stirling's Texas ranch. Self-described podcast host Alice Levine has a lot of questions about whether he's reliable for the job or should, perhaps, be in an aged care facility. I say, fly on, Virgil! Keep cloudsurfing through those beautiful Texas skies.

Rocky's Comment;
Virgil loves flying helicopters which is just as well as he doesn't get much time to do anything else. Jim Stirling is a busy man and he pays Virgil extremely well for his talents. I just wish Virgil could meet Hazel sometime soon... I'm sure she'd quickly enhance his "re entry" landing skills.

103. The Ritz waiter;

One minute pliss. When confronted by an overly expositional customer, this guy didn't know what to do. I say he needs to work on his confidence. Given how quickly people in this world of Belinda Blinked progress up the career ladder, he could be Chancellor of the Exchequer within six months if he put his mind to it.

Rocky's Comment;
Anyone eating out in London will have had this experience. Many excellent waiters from all over the world spend at least six months in this capital city honing their business skills. At the same time, they're improving their English. This means they'll be able to converse with all the English speaking tourists, who will tip them very well, when they return home to open their own restaurant. Fact!

102. The factory orgy participants;

I'm lumping them all together for the sake of brevity...
George Mackintosh,
Neal McDuff,
a packaging engineer,
a burly colander puncher,
et al.
Here's hoping more unions will start advocating that workplaces adopt the morale-boosting atmosphere of the Steele's factory. Sure, more focus on security over sexuality might help protect their trade secrets, but you can't have everything.

Rocky's Comment;
In industry it's pretty normal practice for the sales team to be located miles away from the factory. That's what makes any trip to the factory so exciting. New people to meet, putting faces to names which have previously only been on email lists and so on. Being based in Scotland the homeland of many great engineers, the Steeles Pots and Pans factory employs many locals and with such traditional names like George Mackintosh and Neal McDuff how could they not succeed in making the Tri Oxy Brillo range? Anyone for Haggis?

101. The useless air person;

Belinda's long-haul flight to Australia was ruined by her spat with this klutz, who spilt a drink down our International Sales Director's back. Yet if every hero has a tragic flaw, it could be said that Belinda's admirable confidence can occasionally tend toward arrogance. And it's rare that someone is able to knock her down a peg. So maybe we should applaud this moment of humility as one of the pivotal points in our heroine's progress?

Rocky's Comment;
Humility is not one of the words ever used in the Belinda Blinked books, so it's quite nice that it at least gets an airing in this one. Of course, everyone has had a tangle with someone who has spilt a drink down their back, or even their front... don't mention Bella. But yes, I do agree that these sort of occurrences help in a strange way to develop character and in this case make Belinda a better person... Did I just write that, because as we all know, Belinda is of course perfect.

100. Chi-Chi the Parrot;

We never met Belinda's late lamented parrot, but he has been mentioned on numerous occasions, and was commemorated in a photo on her desk. (Back when she had a desk. Too soon?) Even the FBI's star agent, Helga, was aware of Belinda's penchant for sharing her secrets with Chi-Chi. Could the bird's origin story be more important than we realise? Probably not, but jus' hopin...

Rocky's Comment;
Chi Chi is actually a "lady" parrot with a wicked temper and very sharp beak. Heaven help anyone who gets in the way of her birdseed. But she does talk and that of course was one of the main reasons Belinda acquired her when she left Harolds of Knightsbridge and worked for the Australian clothing conglomerate, International Clothing Pty, selling birdseed....
sorry,
beach clothing... thongs;
beach footwear... thongs;
and classy underwear... thongs.

99. Dick Van Dyke;

Humming alone by the loos in heaven... before his time. Perhaps the aptly-named Dick was also sent back to us to fulfill some supremely important sales-based errands? At time of writing, this respected star has spent seven decades on stage and screen, and I'm sure he'd agree this is his career highlight.

Rocky's Comment;
At number 99 in the rankings, I do sincerely hope Dick Van Dyke makes it past this milestone. His inclusion was the result of once again indulging in way too much 19 Crimes Australian Chardonnay when I should have known better. The good news is, Dick has been real swell about it. What a great guy and genuine example to all the puny, pathetic pricks in Belinda Blinked!

98. The Other Executive(s);

These attractive gents staying at the Stirling In-House Business Hotel were big fans of Steele's, but they may be the only men Belinda and Bella have ever met without sex following immediately thereon. Sorry, guys; it must've been the after-effects of the dehydration from all that hanky-panky in B3.

Rocky's Comment;
This scenario is based on fact. Many large US organisations have a hotel facility built next door to their mega offices. The Tyre companies of the rust belt come particularly to mind. It also makes complete sense, convenience, healthy food, cheap alcohol, conviviality and the ability to bug all the bedrooms meaning you find out what your suppliers are really up to. Jim Stirling being the consummate professional businessman that he is had Belinda and Bella under close surveillance from the moment they checked in. The good news was he liked what he saw and of the course the rest is history.

97. Giselle's sex-starved Dutch-slash-Belgian mother;

We didn't get to hear her speak during her brief appearance at the ill-fated wedding. But Mrs. Maarschalkerweerd de Klotz is responsible for much of what is great about the books: not only is she the progenitor of Giselle's genital disease but one could argue the entire second trilogy would not have happened without her weird illness. I doubt that the International Crockery Association (you know, the ICA) will allow Giselle to keep the spoils of her evil deeds. So, let's hope the Asses and Donkeys Trust can spare some funds. Please help.

Rocky's Comment;
I always hate killing off a strong character, especially when they are surrounded by the mystery which Matilda, Giselle's mother, is. Her genital disease has prompted much debate in many medical circles around the world and as such I can confidentially state that a cure is on its way. Unfortunately, it will come too late for her.

96. Ethel;

Ethel originally appeared as the thinnish tea-lady at Shakespeare's distribution hub, but somehow she has now found herself at Steele's, even gamely participating in the odd group sex party. Just a slip of the pen by Rocky? Or a subtle clue? (Probably the former.) Either way, how can you hate someone whose information is this good, and who's so generous with her beef flaps?

Rocky's Comment;

I have to assume "beef flaps" are an Australian expression, so I'll let that one stand Sammy. But Ethel's move to Steeles near Heathrow airport was a happy serendipity moment. Stan, her husband, is an engine technician for British Jets and he got moved down to Heathrow. Ethel was obviously looking for work and put out some feelers to Belinda and bam!!! she was in employment that next week. So, you see, making friends with the most unlikely of strangers and doing them a good turn can advance your life in ways you'd never imagine. She also enjoys a bit of a group sex party... and organises the Steeles employees summer trip to the seaside.

95. Thick-rimmed glasses (Edmund) and his colleague ("Lunchbreaks");

The problem with having only one photocopier in such a large office building is that you need to have someone to keep up with that endless workload. And ol' mate Edmund was clearly overworked because he turned out to be a damp squib, sex-wise, falling asleep mere moments after coitus with Belinda. Edmund and his inquisitive colleague were yet further opportunities for Jamie to wheel out his dubious spins on a German accent, and he didn't disappoint. (His colleague was wrong however: lunchbreaks turned out not to be Bisch Herstellung's biggest problem.)

Rocky's Comment;
This was a key moment in the search for information as to whether Giselle was guilty or not... but it was Edmund's devotion to his sexual desires which gave Belinda the opportunity to find the evidence... hidden in a small pink file... where else are all the best sexual secrets kept? However, it was a perfect example of sexual opportunity/brilliance by Belinda and Edmund needs to count himself very lucky to have had that encounter... one wonders whether he actually remembered anything at all when he eventually awoke. It's also deemed good business practice to have a centralised photocopying system. Think of all the cost needed to supply every office with their own machine. I know Steeles do it that way, but here's something they could adopt and save a lot of money. Bish isn't stupid when it comes to efficiencies in the workplace. Continuing this line of thought, "Lunchbreaks" is completely correct, imagine the increase in job productivity if no one took a lunchbreak... staggering.

94. Norman Asquith OBE;

A city banker whom Belinda meets at the Duchess' Epsom pile, Norman hasn't contributed in any meaningful way to the story or the sex. But he deserves points for the name alone. When Belinda is done with the cookware industry, I can see her making a rise in the world of big business. Wall Street would love her to bits.

Rocky's Comment;
Norman Asquith OBE was present at the dinner to meet Sir James Godwin. As a City of London financier he was uniquely placed to place large sums of money in Sir James' way, thereby financing his Pots and Pans company. It takes contacts to get on in the world of business and Belinda quickly realised this. You have to give her ten out of ten for effort, even with those bullets churning away inside her.

93. Doc Al;

This Australian flying doctor, with a garden salad for a head, is exceptionally unusual. His unfinished PhD on prehensile toes is certainly a noble area in which to specialise. And he's figured out a shortcut from the Australian outback to the heart of Sydney, a path which claimed the morale and lives of countless 19th century explorers. But I simply can't endorse rimming someone who's been three days in the desert. Under almost any circumstances.

Rocky's Comment;
This is a very special character for me. Years ago I remember watching the flying doctor on television and this is my nod to their bravery and professionalism. I also love dropping in the odd musical reference in the Belinda Blinked books and this is one such example. "Call me Al" is one of Paul Simon's brilliant pieces of music and if you've not seen the clip on You Tube of him with Chevvy Chase you should check it out. Also watch out for the musical instrument falling through the table. Another one to view on You Tube is Paul Simon's concert in Hyde Park, London in 2014... his rapport with the other musicians is amazing when singing this song! So when the Aussie flying doc says to Belinda, "Call me Al" I just love it.

92. Bobby Blumenthal;

We haven't met Blumenthal *père* yet, but he taught Belinda everything she knows and also remained married to her... unorthodox mother, for all these years, so he must be pretty inspiring. One assumes he didn't know about the Three B Tree, or he mightn't have encouraged his daughter to become quite the kitchenware powerhouse she did.

Rocky's Comment;
Bobby Blumenthal, wine merchant of some repute, Sommelier of fine wines and father to Belinda Bounty Blumenthal. What a man, what a family and you have to admire how he happily imparts his business sales tips to his daughter. Well, some of them at any rate... Keep drinking the wine Mr. Blumenthal... Oh btw, what are your thoughts on the 19 Crimes Chard from Australia?

91. Footman at Harold's of London;

This is all in Jamie's performance, but this cameo role in one of the Christmas specials is an absolute treat. Harold's Emporium offers an enviable range of products from lockdown survival catering to limited-edition-festively-wrapped-upon-purchase sex implements, and this footman has an encyclopaedic knowledge of them all. If only all Jamie's voices were this brief.

Rocky's Comment;
A small role for a big man. I say big man because he's basically a bouncer as he's stationed there to avoid any riff raff from entering this prestigious store in central London. The fact that he's got an encyclopaedic mind for every item sold in the store... and knows where it's located, indicates to me that he's more than just a footman. I would hazard a guess that he's some form of internal security, fending off the shoplifters on an hourly basis. This man has got potential.

90. Geoffrey Drabble and Henry Babble;

Two-thirds of Dribble, Drabble, and Babble, Forensic Accountants, the elderly Geoffrey handles the networking side of the business (he's often seen at Ascot with our dear Duchess) while Henry is a renowned tech expert, who even writes his own code. Appearing so far only in *Lockdown 69*, these top-notch analysts were able to salvage Steele's' assets before they could be whisked away to an East German bank account. Expect to see them assisting COCK again in the future.

Rocky's Comment;
I couldn't resist the company name, Dribble, Drabble and Babble... it's somehow so evocative of what their firm actually does... or rather, doesn't do. They certainly don't dribble, they don't drabble and they never babble. Having close ties to MI6, these guys appreciate the delicate nature of international theft and the means law enforcement has to go to solving the crime. The fact they've been around a long time brings a note of responsibility and sobriety to their clandestine accountancy investigations. I'd keep their number in your phone book... you never know when you might need them.

89. The Ranch Crew (Chuck and Doug);

These Texan farmhands really would make a great band. They're impressively adept at the difficult art of swimming pool sex, without the need to pre-dock. And that bitter taste of nicotine, tequila, and beer will haunt my dreams… for the rest of my life.

Rocky's Comment;
These guys are bit part players. Itinerant Texan workers who just happened to strike it lucky when Belinda and Bella turned up at the Lazy P ranch one glorious hot afternoon. I doubt if they could even ride a horse never mind herd a bunch of cattle across Texas. Luckily for them they could swim.

88. Miguel the waiter;

Serving drinks at a hotel on the Costa del Sol, Miguel's lack of cunnilingus training is evident, unfortunately. But he's clearly got the raw material. As tourism revives after covid, I pray that the Spanish Tourist Board will pay for the required training and get Miguel to the place he needs to be.

Rocky's Comment;

Yes, Miguel is on the up and working for a top notch Spanish hotel on the Costa del Sol strip is a good indicator of where he is right now in his career. It's quite obvious to me that he'll soon be in London fine tuning his waiter skills. Perhaps even getting that extra bit of professional training he's sorely lacking, before returning to Spain and setting up his own beach side bar. Hey Miguel, mines a big jug of cold Sangria!

87. Dave Wilcox;

The unseasoned reader might hear the name "Dave Wilcox" and think "how depressingly bland". But you'd be surprised to learn that it's actually another sign of pure Rocky brilliance. Stellar performances (in every sense of that word) don't just come from the Chiara Montagues of the world, after all. Rocky has always been a champion of that classic figure of English drama, the everyman. Dave remains the least-developed of the RSMs, but his dense dick made quite the impression in book six. In *Lockdown 69*, Dave's real talent was revealed. He proved himself so exceptional at masturbating a lady that the Duchess made plans to poach him from Steele's! Great things may lie ahead for Mr. Wilcox.

Rocky's Comment;
Dave Wilcox has always struggled to retain his place in the RSM's team. But from time to time, he does get a chance to shine and one of my favourites was in the HBO special where he was the local man at the team building session in Cornwall. It was his role to keep the lid on things before they got out of hand. The results of those few days speak for themselves, but at least he at last became a team player. Keep trying Dave, you'll get there eventually... perhaps you should ask Belinda to visit some of your customers, after all you could do with the extra sales.

86. Cornelius Kettle;

Cornelius Kettle may not be especially friendly or forward-thinking... how could he dismiss Belinda's emphatic presentation, with her innovative idea of promoting a brand by featuring it on a television program? But what he lacks in sales savvy, he clearly makes up for as a talent agent, having shepherded his celebrity client through 324 episodes of *Cooking with Cosmo*, and at least one season of that international sensation, *Dance in the Sky with Superstars*. "Cornelius Kettle" might just win the prize for most inspired character name of the series.

Rocky's Comment;
CK is basically a slob who makes a very good living on other people's efforts. The fact he snubbed Belinda's advances shows how much he just doesn't care. Very much true to real life, what else should we expect from a professional agent. But he is successful and after 15 seasons of Cooking with Cosmo, we do have to give him grudging respect... well perhaps.

85. The service station attendant;

Let's all be sympathetic to this unruly and randy young man, who was offered an unsolicited presentation on female anatomy while he filled up Belinda's car. His fellow unwashed peasants down the pub are gonna love it.

Rocky's Comment;
To be honest, I was a service station attendant of a similar age and I always dreamed of this happening to me. It never did... perhaps because I didn't work weekends, well up to 12 noon on a Saturday. Never mind, at least I was able to relive it through Belinda and the Duchess. Now that was certainly more exciting than the seventy plus year old biddys I used to fill up.

84. The Hunts Girls;

Doris, Joan, and their two sisters, who provided striptease entertainment for the randy mob at Steele's Xmas Party. Why are they octogenarian strippers, to quote Alice Levine, who inexplicably dress like they're going fox hunting? Did Cedric provide their services along with Belinda's horse-riding outfit? (Perhaps they're his sisters...) Why are they bewilderingly concerned about other people being nosy? Or is that just the answer women like to give Des Martin? All these questions and more will likely never be answered, but isn't that exactly the reason we love Rocky's bananas approach to character development?

Rocky's Comment;
Thank you, Sammy... I do feel I should answer some of your questions and I'll start with the fox hunting outfits. It was all Belinda's idea, she wanted a segway to the future, especially as there is no doubt, they are so sexy. Mind you the fox probably doesn't think so. Cedric was of course the supplier and no doubt had a good Christmas lunch on the back of the sales, but they aren't related. As to them being nosy, these are professional artistes and have every right to their privacy... as do we all!!! jus sayin...

83. Benny, Bella's brother;

Given the rest of his family, it's no surprise that Benny, Bella's Brother, has an IQ at the lowest end of the spectrum, but he earns back some points for that veiny milky bar. As we learned in *Lockdown 69*, this description of his pasteurised phallus is apt: Benny is a key member of the British milk industry. He even comes complete with his own milk float for all your transportation needs. I agree with the podcast team, though, that someone wearing a nightcap to bed can never possibly be sexy. (Will we ever meet his sister Pamela? She's not worth the paper to describe, apparently, although when has that, ever stopped Rocky?)

Rocky's Comment;
Benny Bella's Brother is another potential 3B candidate. His name is so suited to the spy industry I'm surprised he hasn't been recruited to MI6 by the Duchess. Of course, he may already be in their employ and he's working under deep cover as an inner London milkman. It's probably about time Belinda checked his milk bottle tops for bugs and other spyware. The fact he wears a nightcap to bed gives a lot more credence to that idea... if James Sp00ner kept his devices strapped to his ankle, why can Benny Bella's Brother not have them stuck on his head?

82. Mrs Huddlesbird;

Belinda's grade 3 bassoon teacher, sadly deceased. There's no evidence that Belinda kept up her bassoon training, although we've seen evidence of her fantastic skills as an actress and also her impressive singing abilities in an impromptu duet (in Portuguese, no less!) with Señor Zip. (Not to mention her haunting lyric poetry about TWGU Union official Andy Milstone.) So perhaps Mrs Huddlesbird will be more appreciated in the afterlife. Our loss is the Heaven Symphony Orchestra's gain.

Rocky's Comment;
Amen.

81. Jim Walters;

This security expert from Apollo Security Agencies met Belinda at Epsom Hall, where she was intoxicated by his professional experience. Jim's only contribution to the narrative thus far has to been to provide the services of James Sp00ner. In light of Sp00ns' job performance, I have to wonder if Jim decided to pocket the fee for himself and send in a cheap substitute. Yes, Jimmy Walters has some questions to answer.

Rocky's Comment;

Another member of the Chicken Kiev poisoning scandal at Epsom Hall where the Duchess resides when she's not working full blast in London central. It seems to me that whilst the Duchess was playing love eggs with Belinda's vagina, she was also introducing her to some pretty important contacts for the future. Jim Walters came to her aide fairly quickly with the recruitment of Sp00ns, but we also may be seeing Norman Asquith OBE utilised as Belinda starts to grow her new empire. A bit of dosh goes a long, long, way in East Germany, especially British Pounds against East German Marks.

80. Quince;

There were so many warning signs. Why did he claim to have come from "Jim Jim Falls", which famously had no water flowing over it? Why did he willingly sit anywhere near Bella Ridley? And what kind of a name is Quince? Unfortunately, we were lured in by the carefree appeal of this Spanish backpacker until he betrayed us all, took his five measly bucks, and disappeared into the Australian wilderness. I hope it was worth it, Hombre.

Rocky's Comment;
I hate Quince... that's why I named him such. In actual fact a Quince is a bitter sweet small apple used for making jam. Of course, you have to add a lot of sugar to the mush to make it edible. In other words, they're pretty useless. It was a pity Belinda and Bella didn't see his bitterness before they were betrayed. I also doubt he was Spanish... well if he was, he was from Venezuela or somewhere close by... not the real Spain.

79. Hazel the [co-] pilot;

One of the most proficient pilots the world has ever known? Sure. Equally as competent flying a jumbo jet full of passengers as she is soaring across the Bay of Biscay in a 1950s de Havilland transport plane stuffed with weekend editions of the *Guardian* magazine? True. Able to tell the time down to the second no matter how dark it is because of her massive, fluorescent watch? Yeah, okay. Still, she's just an encumbrance on our freewheeling gal pals, and if they'd just invited Maeve to the hen's (bachelorette party) instead of Hazel, so much might have been different. Get in the fucking sea.

Rocky's Comment;
I love Hazel in the same way I hate Quince. Hazel is someone who facilitates Belinda's way through life. Imagine if we all had a private pilot to count on... why I'd be in Sydney tomorrow and London the day after. But hey wait... Belinda's new role as CEOO of the old Bisch Herstellung may just call for such a person. Anyways Sammy, what've you got against the distribution of the weekend Guardian supplements throughout Southern Spain? I mean this is spreading Anglo Saxon culture at its best!

78. Norm from next door;

The Ridleys' next-door neighbour, with his Rudolph mask and stone-wash denim jeans, is almost transcendentally macabre. Bella jumps him every Christmas Eve, but I'm not sure if that's one for the pro... or the con... column.

Rocky's Comment;
Norm is to me as the ranch cowboys Chuck and Hank are to Jim Stirling... necessary but deadbeats. However, I do like his stone wash denim... I have a great shirt in exactly the same material, so he can't be all bad.

77. Sydney the PA;

A savvy assistant at the Stirling Organisation, Sydney's interests include well-formatted schedules (you know, itineraries?), bikini bottoms, and punching that twelfth! She was rather overshadowed by the more salacious events during Belinda and Bella's stay in Texas. Also, she could've told the two B's that Jim wasn't in town before they arranged their meet-and-greet...

Rocky's Comment;

Ahh... but that's the point, Sydney knew Jim would be flying in that night and that he was on a tight schedule and that he wanted some time with Belinda. After all he had a lot to get through, so to speak, in the new cock department. What with his blue jizz and flaking skin he was probably feeling a bit under confident. However, Sydney did her best to scare off the English gals but was she working under orders or out of self-interest. Somehow, I think we'll be seeing more of Ms. Sydney. But it was great to see them all become friends at the BBQ the next day... business moves in mysterious ways.

76. The BB3 commentators;

Providing multilingual and well-researched commentary on the funeral of the "Much Honoured James Sp00ner, Laird of Gretna Green", these erudite journalists had cameo appearances only, but perfectly conveyed the atmosphere inside Westminster Abbey for that most solemn of events. How lucky they were to be able to hear that fantastic eulogy delivered personally by Her Majesty Queen Lizzie 2. (Yes, the monarch was at the funeral, but even from my far-flung corner of the Empire, I'm not bold enough to include her on the list.)

Rocky's Comment;

Gretna Green is in Scotland and I visited it many years ago... not that, I hasten to add, I was marrying someone, that happened many years later, but to visit the local fish and chip shop. I'm sure Sp00ner visited the same one every time he was up North on official duties as the Laird. That means Lord in English and a great title it is too. As to the commentators it was nice to be able to make sure that most of what they said barely told the truth. Classic journo's... give them a snippet of information and they'll make a great story out of it.

75. Natasha Biles and Samantha Jones;

The two newest members of the Confidential Order of Cookware Knights (er... COCK) are initiated in *Lockdown 69*. Their sensitively-depicted initiation ritual is enhanced by a traditional Amazonian potion only available to licensed medical practitioners. Natasha is a bit hesitant in the ways of love, although her inhibitions are considerably loosened after a couple of days with the Steele's team. Welsh Samantha (whose name may or may not be stolen from *Sex and the City?*) is always up for it, and she comes with added extras in the form of an array of tattoos and a luscious collection of body piercings (three on each lid!). I can't believe it took so long for Steele's to organise some sales training for its staff. Maybe the company's fortunes will turn around after all.

Rocky's Comment;
As training gurus... refer to the HBO special, Natasha and Samantha are fantastic characters to write with. The second half of the training days in Cornwall has yet to be published, but there we start to understand why Natasha is a bit reticent about picking up the Steeles Pots and Pans account a second time (Bella has a lot to do with it). Nevertheless, beggars can't be choosers and with the able assistance of her new colleague Samantha, Natasha is soon back into the saddle. It was also about time I got into writing about tats and piercings and after some personal research I felt quite comfortable on the subject. It's interesting that in the less creative universe, tattoos and such aren't as well accepted by the hierarchies of big business and are perhaps one of the major reasons Belinda and the Glee Team don't indulge too much. However, Belinda's 3B's tattoo does point to some liberal thinking in her earlier life. The good news is Sammy, you'll meet these two once again in the near future.

74. The McDonagh brothers;

Is it weird that I'm jealous of Giselle? These Irish businessmen... Kevin, Danny, and Sean... gave her a good time... albeit it descended into fisticuffs when they fought over who got to enjoy which hole. Ma McDonagh will surely have some questions about their black eyes when they next pop around for tea. Not only do they perform a magnificently harmonised version of *Will Ye Go, Lassie, Go*, but they were there for the first time we learned about Giselle's good-sex alopecia. If anyone deserves a rosette, it's these boys.

Rocky's Comment;
I'm still amazed I've not been able to get Belinda to visit their company and do some business... surely, they'd be up for a bit of standard sex in exchange for a few thousand units order? What's more embarrassing is that they hail from the same country as I do? Perhaps I'm a bit afraid the "boys" might pop around and continue their fist fight with me being the punch ball? Or maybe Belinda's seen through their little game... they go to all the corporate days out but don't have any decision making clout? Perhaps we'll never find out... But yes, they can sing and Will ye go Lassie, Go, is one of my favourites, having first heard it sang by a drunken group of 4 Irishmen in a Donegal Town pub... a great night! Note the musical reference just crowbarred into the story?

73. Dr Veronica Studd;

How do we feel about Dr. Studd? On the one hand, she's somehow carved out a career as a female doctor (can you imagine?). And, despite being an unconscious specialist (she's only responsible until the second they wake up), she still finds time to moonlight as a sex therapist. On the other hand, Alice's concern about this doctor's ethical stance must be taken seriously. Whether it's seducing hospital visitors or allowing bottles of Chardonnay to languish by her comatose patients' beds, Veronica has never seen a rule she wouldn't bypass. If it weren't for James Cooper's disturbingly alluring voice for the character, I'd be calling for the medical board to revoke her license.

Rocky's Comment;

I thoroughly enjoyed writing this character. It was a great feeling leading James and Alice (and all you guys out there) up the garden path by you all assuming Dr Studd was a male. A classic perception turned on its head in one word. Credit due to Jamie… he didn't give the game away which made it doubly rewarding for us all.

But hey Sammy… what's all the fuss about Veronica doing a bit of moonlight work as a sex therapist? All good Dr's do a bit of work trying their best to reduce backlogs of false hips, wonky knees and so on. So keep it up Docs… we need you!

FYI I have another book series, as yet unpublished, where Dr Veronica in her day job does work as a sex therapist…

72. The Bothy Man;

This elderly gent in the Scottish Cairngorms tried his best to help our heroines recover their body temperature after an avalanche. Strangely, they weren't that interested. Was he involved in the unusual babushka-style fuckfest that ended the chapter? The jury remains out on that one.

Rocky's Comment;
Being Judge and Jury on this one I can quite categorically confirm the keeper of the Bothy was no way involved in his overnight guests' private tastes. No, hard working staff, such as this chap, can be well relied upon to keep their mouths shut and the alcohol flowing. Yes, it was indeed his private store of illegal vintage "Bothy Whiskey" which kept the lassies warm through that long night.

71. Chantelle;

This lightly-dressed chanteuse… as bald as a Crenshaw melon… seems to be on a downhill trajectory, career-wise (a stage in the corner of a club in Amsterdam's 'Red Light District' doesn't sound promising). As much as I enjoy sexy versions of 1960s laidback jazz classics (boop-boop-be-do), it might be time for some new material. Personally, though? I'm a fan. *Plus de chansons*, Chantelle!

Rocky's Comment;
I love Chantelle's take on life and the job. Working for Countess Zara would not be an easy choice… one wrong note, one miss step… well you'd fall off the stage… and you could find yourself working one of the upstairs bedrooms albeit with a plaster cast on the broken leg. But this gal is pluckier than that, she knows that one day her hero will walk into that club and as has been written before, "where in all the clubs in all the world did I find you…"
Keep singing Chantelle, I just love a bit of Herb Alpert and of course there's another musical reference!

70. Mr Hushman;

One of the most singularly bizarre figures in the narrative thus far. A background goon with a voice so high some dogs wouldn't be able to hear it. Hushman is a big guy with a small back... however that works. Hushman enjoys attending kinky fetish parties dressed in a full mouse costume, complete with buckteeth, and could be found lying on his back in the Couples' Cave of Cuddles, waiting for pleasure. Somehow (don't ask me how, since I'm pretty sure Giselle forgot to steal them), he managed to pocket the blueprints to the Tri-Oxy-Brillo range, leading to a death that was as hideous and unwelcome as literally everything else about him.

Rocky's Comment;
Yeah... Hushman is one of the kinkier of the books many varied characters... but to be honest, they were in East Berlin and I suspect he was trying to pretend he was a real Berliner... he just got the Bugs Bunny teeth wrong. Do East Berliners have big tails? I'm also surprised he actually made it so high into the rankings, I mean, beating Drrrr Studdddd and the Welsh Training Wizards... wow that is a big call, Sammy?

<u>69 (heh). Monty Jim the Pizza Boy;</u>

This horny, blonde 19-year-old isn't exactly a world-leading intellect. He might not be all that fit, either, because it took him a full 10 minutes to climb six flights of stairs... although it might have been all that time trying to navigate the warren of penthouses on Belinda's floor. Still, by stripping off at the first sign of a naked customer, Monty Jim the Pizza Boy is living a classic porn trope, and you've gotta respect that.

Rocky's Comment;
Classic porn tropes are the rage where I live these days and it seems to me that you have to be under the age of 22 to be counted in that tribe. Once again no one's noticed I've inserted yet another James... well Jim, into the overcrowded world of Belinda Blinked. But getting back to the tropes, that's a good thing because I've nailed my colours to the mast by using the number 69 to my advantage... I also like 56, but who's counting? Belinda's penthouse is also numbered 69 and some people have mistakenly taken that to mean she lives on the 69th floor. Unfortunately, that is incorrect because there are 69 units in the complex of which... surprisingly, No. 69 is the only penthouse on top of the rest... think of a pyramid type building. Simple ehh?
Oh, by the way due to her new responsibilities in East Germany Belinda has put the penthouse up for sale, here's the advert;

Three Bed Penthouse Apartment for Sale; Starting Price £2,950,000
Owner may consider renting to suitable foreign power. (references required)
69 Half Moon Street. London.W1J 7AZ
Central London location; Just 5 minutes from Mayfair;

Sole Selling Agents; Hurst, Blumenthal & Burt;

Unique opportunity to purchase a stunning roof top residence just minutes from Green Park Tube Station with its excellent transport facilities; Located on the edge of the International Embassy district with all its Government security. Underground car parking for 4+ cars;

Property description;

A luxurious top floor apartment (with 2 lifts and private spiral staircase) situated within a period building of Edwardian distinction, close to Park Lane. The property comprises hallway, reception room leading to magnificent roof terrace, granite finished kitchen, magnificent master bedroom with en suite and waterbed (to be negotiated), 2nd double bedroom en suite, 3rd single bedroom, bathroom/shower room with wooden flooring, 24 hour concierge and parking for 4+ vehicles.
Stunning 6th floor City of London views; South-West facing aspect; Topiary Gardens with private BBQ and Hot Tub area.
Secure Large Underground Parking and Long Leasehold
Read more at hurstblumenthalburt.co.uk/for-sale/details/4069

68. Jim Thompson;

The Mr. Fix-it of Steele's, the glee team have hinted that Jim likes men, which would make him a rare openly queer male character in the Blumiverse. For the most part, though, he's been reduced to brief mentions and forgettable interactions... which is fair, since he's failed to fix literally anything thus far. In *Lockdown 69*, at long last, we learned that 58-year-old Jim was on to his fourth wife (Peggy Strumpethouse, if you must know) until their South Sea Island honeymoon was ruined by first, a covid lockdown, and second, the reveal that she wasn't quite who she said she was. Never mind. Jim impressed us all with his ability to rapidly rebound. Hopefully Jim's back in London now, since his driving is apparently the only way to transport someone to and from the airport, given the outrageous taxi situation at Heathrow!

Rocky's Comment;
I'm going to make a statement...
"When I worked in London at an office not far from the Steeles Offices... we shared the same carpark, it was fact that you could not get a taxi from Heathrow Airport to the office in West Drayton. It was a very simple reason... the journey was too short and the fare too low to justify the cab being in a queue for 40 minutes for a 10 minute, at best, fare."
...End of Statement.
Jim Thompson is based on a gentleman who did work at these same offices doing a similar job as Jim. I have changed the names to protect the innocent, but he did a fantastic job and without people with this sort of dedication we would not have the fantastic international companies we have in London today! Well done all the Jim Thompsons out there... we need you!!

67. Madeleine Chocolat;

Well-known for her chocolate empire (that's not what you think it is), Madeleine's masculine air can't be ignored, nor her Willy Wonka vibes. Should there be swimming and love-making in the product? Is it practical to transport viscous chocolate across the globe? Does Chocolate Cholate's bespoke business model make any practical sense? Well, far be it from me to argue with the people of Californicatia.

Rocky's Comment;
I unfortunately love chocolate, so does Wilma… add a touch of orange to mine and I'm in so called Heaven, Wilma likes it plain and brown… like her men… well I do try. So as such it was very pleasant to include a character such as Madeleine Chocolat into the story. I was only disappointed in one thing the guys didn't cotton onto… in France a Madeleine is a little bun, with orange overtones and is beautiful with some melted chocolate to dip into… am I setting a very sexy image here??? Probably not… I'll stick to porn.

66. Andy Milston;

Oh, Andy. You desperate, creepy, professionally conflicted man. When you're not staring directly into the employees' canteen at Shakespeare Retail Stores, you're gathering a collection of locks of women's hair. I hope you figure out how to respect women one day, and then perhaps you'll see your wife's tits again. But I won't hold my breath. Give him a company pen and be done with it.

Rocky's Comment;

Andy Milston is a very misunderstood man. But he is still a man, and a big personal friend of Ken Dewsbury. He also works closely with Matilda in accounts letting her know when Ken is visiting so she can get him to check out the wrong invoices Steeles have sent her over the last month. I feel sorry for Ken, this is the worst part of the job for a creative, fast talking salesman... sorting out dull old invoices which no one understands apart from Matilda and Peggy Strumpethouse back in London. I also feel sorry for Andy, a man who loves his work. Placed in middle management in a highly motivated company... I do envy him getting a visit from Belinda Blumenthal from Steeles Pots and Pans... wow, he must have been on laxatives for a full week before her visit.

65. Fanny Driller;

She may only have one scene but this Australian lady-of-the-evening proved to be a talented power bottom and someone with a keen interest in state politics. She was also the last shag Sp00ner ever had. For that she will never be forgotten. (Except by the Government of the United Kingdom, which failed to invite her to his state funeral.)

Rocky's Comment;
Sammy... what the fuck is she not doing here??? And that was probably the question everyone was asking at the funeral. Talk about bit parts... this has to be one of the best... an illusion, an insinuation... everything apart from an actual manifestation of the human body... #65... I ask you?

64. Digby Dodd;

This co-pilot from Bolton isn't especially warm (although *I'd* be suspicious of Belinda on first sight) but he knows when to throw caution to the wind and join a shagfest. Even while flying a plane full of people over the Indian Ocean. Leaving unguarded the button which sends the vessel on a non-stop trajectory to Mars. Yeah, let's not ask too many questions.

Rocky's Comment;
Digby has flown aircraft for many years now and never been investigated by the Civil Aviation Authority... based in the UK. So, when you get the opportunity to let your hair down with a couple of lovely girls halfway across the Indian Ocean, you gotta join in. I do think we're all lucky Bella was in Economy class, or Belinda might have blinked for her last time.

63. The Belgian Butler;

Avancez! This Belgian Butler is lucky his job hasn't been automated yet, frankly. I mean, couldn't they just set a timer on someone's smartphone? Or set up one of those aggressive honking horns used by school sports days? But I suppose someone needs to sign the driver's delivery form to send all of those clothes and personal belongings off to charity. God bless the European spirit.

Rocky's Comment;

This Belgian Butler called Bertie... have you noticed the thing?? Sorry... I'm going to do something about this "B" thing... honestly. But what a wonderful job... think of all the little trinkets kept in the pockets of those discarded clothes... rings, phones, wallets and best of all... address books... well the address list in the phone! Phew... Belgian Bertie could be into a big blackmailing racket when he gets the sack from his current job. Make a wonderful story... jus thinkin...

62. Aldo Fellini;

This Italian businessman (don't *you* shop at Inca Supermercatos SpA?) didn't get much screentime during his brief appearance in the Reading Room. On his return in *Lockdown 69*, however, he couldn't keep his hands... or his extremities... to himself for a moment. If I'm honest, he sounds fiiiine, and I sure envy that medium-length haircut.

Rocky's Comment;
Aldo is a wonderful sexy Italiano hunk whom Belinda just can't get to visit for all the reasons in the world. For now, he's joined the Dave Wilcox club... in the wings... waiting for his big scene. I hope it comes soon for his sake... before it's too late and Belinda stops Blinking at him.

61. Peggie Strumpethouse;

Jim Thompson's fourth wife, and formerly a member of the Steele's accounting team, Peggie revealed herself in *Lockdown 69* to be unreliable. Her mission was to infiltrate Steele's without their knowing, join a conspiracy to defraud the company of millions, marry Jim, follow her two co-conspirators to the South Seas, gain the information, deal with them and the rest is in Lockdown 69....

Rocky's Comment;
What a wonderful character... full of venom, treachery, deceit and completely ruthless... but so loving Jim Thompson married her. One has to wonder did she attend the Gerramima St Frostfurst school of acting otherwise known as RADS... explained in detail later. Working in accounts it's obvious that she's sharp with numbers... too sharp, but that's the cookie life throws at you. This lady has a lot further to go... in many ways.

60. Gloria Ridley;

Who doesn't love a constant whine of Christmas songs? Bella's loving mother is the over caring, over catering type we all need when we're invited to a friend's Christmas do, and the autotuning in Jamie's voice has never been so fine.

Rocky's Comment;
Bella's parents own a pub, known as a boozer in this Xmas Special. It's really hard work, but it's the love, joy and song which Gloria brings to her business and clients that makes her such a great parent to Bella, though Arty her husband no doubt does his best. Anyone who has to make 200 pigs in blankets on Xmas Eve deserves to be in these rankings, though Arty only gets to #107. He must have been putting out the Monopoly sets. Oh... a pig in blanket is a sausage rolled in a piece of bacon... self-explanatory really!

59. The Minister;

"Dearly beloved..." One of Jamie's most iconic voices, the minister seems to be on his last legs. And those hours spent practising how to pronounce Giselle's surname must have taken their toll. I hope he got to sit down at the reception with a big slice of that artistic-looking wedding cake...

Rocky's Comment;
That voice is so similar to a very beloved comedian called Alan Carr working in the UK. Alan is camp, effeminate and totally irreverent; making this scene work so much better to those who are in the know... as you are now! I hope all his marriages have a better ending than Giselle's and Tony's. Let us pray dearly beloved...

58. Betty Wilks and Vic Woods;

Well-known for their sloppy business attire and love of free booze, these women sent Belinda to the height of her fame at the O2. Sorry, I mean Millennium Dome Building. The mind boggles as to why their attire was so rumpled at the start of their journey. And why they didn't invite Steele's when they were initially organising the conference. And why they needed such a vast group for a fact-finding mission. And what facts exactly, did they expect to find? In fact, nothing about these women makes sense. Lord, I hope their coffee morning business survived the pandemic.

Rocky's Comment;
This is really a homage to the wonderful British comedienne Victoria Wood, known to her friends as Vic. All my family are big fans of her work and her annual Xmas Specials were never to be missed. Thank you, Vic, for the inspiration. I hope she also would have loved the scene in which I set her… a group of boozed up direct sales ladies returning home from a fact finding mission, on behalf of Claus Bloch, in Holland. Crumpled but undeflated… always ready for a top up, the true sign of an entrepreneur.

57. Adaam;

I want to like Forster's chief salesperson more than I do. He's blessed with a dick that's instantly erect and hung like a red London bus, and he expresses a rare scepticism about the attitude of our heroines. Still, you just know he's the kind of guy who keeps his own urine in a jar and plays the ukulele on his balcony at 2 in the morning. What an oddball.

Rocky's Comment;
Yes Sammy, are you referring to your next door neighbour... but I think this one you've got right... Adaam is an oddball... even the way he spells his name makes you wonder if he's got all his marbles... surely no parent would do that to their child. But it was his socks that I was most intrigued with... Belinda was able to smell one of the foremost Irish Whiskeys, namely Bushmills, world famous for their "Black Bush" from his "hose". Her sense of smell was obviously enhanced by her father Bobby Blumenthal. After all it was he who passed on to her his wine tasting skills... smell being one of the most important. More deep back story for those of you who enjoy such things.
As for the "Red London Bus..." what a perfect description and Sammy, you have every right to be jealous!

56. Monty, the Anciently House Master of the Keys;

I feel like this budget version of Dobby had more to offer than we could find the time for. Already highly regarded for his office sandwiches, Monty benefited from Steele's compassionate approach to their underperforming employees to emerge with a title fit for an epic fantasy novel. But if he thought sales was tough, even Monty couldn't have predicted the variety of tasks in his new role; that Steele's Rummikub tournament isn't going to organise itself! I would say that Monty's day is done now that Bisch has been arrested, but knowing Steele's crackpot approach to recruitment he'll probably turn up as the Leather Room maître d' before too long.

Rocky's Comment;
Firstly, 56 is one of my favourite numbers.
Secondly, Monty, the Anciently House Master of the Keys is truly a Dobby character and just as faithful. Even after taking a well-deserved retirement from Steeles Pots and Pans, he was very happy to take on casual visiting work just to keep his ex-office pals in delicious sandwiches. And then things snowballed... as they do in life. He gamely came out of retirement, like so many other oldies, to help stave off the pandemic and help out his old firm. His reward was brutal as Lockdown 69 saw him officiating in a new COCK members initiation ceremony... where next?

55. Zachariah;

This local business owners magic wand offers pleasure to every lady's orifice. Weirdly, that's not a euphemism. Zachariah seems to have emerged fully formed from a Scandinavian folk story, with his mystic dance moves, scintillating robes and the esoteric Taramix flute. I was thinking of moving him up the rankings until I heard 10-year-old James Cooper's passionate anti-drug rap. Drugs are *wrong*, Zachariah (and also sometimes *right*).

Rocky's Comment;
As a night club owner, Zachariah needs to find an angle and blowing very sexy looking cigarette smoke up his biggest fans asses is just the right hook for his business. So, to set all minds at rest, it's not the smoke that debilitates his client base, it's those Desperado's our heroines had consumed all evening. Tequila based drinks have a well established reputation for this sort of thing. So, Zach... I'll be down next weekend... Cheers!

54. Claus Bloch;

This child of young Austrian immigrants is known as a Casanova to his personal friends, and they weren't wrong! The Direct Retail Door to Door and Coffee Morning Organisation's CEO and Managing Director was so gifted that his sexual prowess transformed Belinda into some kind of sabre-toothed tiger, right there in a suite of the Grosvenor Hotel. It's one of the all-time classic chapters, but Claus can't rank higher because his importance to the overall plot is questionable at best.

Rocky's Comment;
I think Claus Bloch's real story is yet untold. The man, no... the legend, who can make Belinda enjoy a sexual liaison so deeply must still be hovering somewhere in her deep subconscious. Now that she's back on an even keel, is it time for Belinda to let her inner soul take her to the man who can so deeply satisfy her craven sexual being. Does he purchase stuff from Bisch Herstellung? Will he do so with Belinda's involvement... or can he stimulate her back to being a dinosaur... all questions we need answering!!

53. The Prime Minister;

I'm not going to make any assumptions about which real-life figure the *Lockdown 69* PM might be based on, but he's chummy with the aristocracy and prone to a needlessly complicated turn of phrase, so I'll leave that to your imagination. More importantly, there's an international spoon shortage, which has in turn led to an ice cream crisis, and this Prime Minister is not going to let his country down, even if it means calling in the loopiest member of the aristocracy and an exceptionally busy pots-and-pans senior saleswoman. Who wouldn't vote for this man?

Rocky's Comment;
Spoondemics have a habit, thankfully, of bringing the right person to the right job at the right time. This applies to MI6 veterans, Prime Ministers and even International Sales Directors. Happily, for us, Belinda was able to bring her own unique and very direct way of doing things to the disaster. By delegating major roles to her own RSM's at Steeles Pots and Pans, major achievements were made in a very short space of time. If only they could be so effective in their "nine to five" day jobs.

52. Patrick "Paddy" O'Hamlin;

Patrick hasn't played much of a role in the books thus far, although to be fair he's managing two entire countries, so probably has less time to play. Nevertheless, he reliably shows up whenever carnal congress is on offer. And let's never forget that time he was able to procure a reindeer just to hang out in the office Christmas grotto. (Keep the reindeer away from the barrel of mead, for god's sake!) Rocky's world is as morally upright as that of Charles Dickens, and I suspect Paddy will prove to be the one truly honourable character of the series, as well as the RSM who will ultimately triumph on the sales hierarchy. That, or Rocky will forget about him entirely. It's a tossup.

Rocky's Comment;
Patrick O'Hamlin is a resourceful sort of chap who loves staying just out of the limelight... but he is one for the girls. The second part of the Training Conference in Cornwall (as yet unpublished) brings him further out of the shadows and with Des Martin, his English born nemesis, sparks start to fly. But being in charge of two countries is a very much normal way of doing business in sales structures. You see it's all based on population count and the Scottish and Irish populations barely number twelve million. Consider Greater London where the population is over ten million and you start to comprehend why these territories exist in the way they do. When you relate this to the sales of pots and pans, much like car tyres, the more people you have, then the more sales you'll achieve... still with me?

51. Norman Togui;

This mysteriously-named figure from the University of London Business School only appeared on Belinda's CV but he has earned an array of fans based on his name alone. Did Rocky have a real-life Norman Togui in mind when he scribbled it down? You can give me a reference any day, Norman.

Rocky's Comment;
Norman Togui is an academic working at the London Business School Campus. One of the foremost business educational establishments in the world, it is no wonder that Belinda found her love of the industry within these walls. Norm himself is a mild-mannered guy born in Chicago USA and now working at the epicentre of business advancement. You see the brain drain can work both ways. It must be said Norm is no relative of Bella's parents next door neighbour also called Norm as depicted in one of the Xmas Specials. It's obviously a really popular name, like James... Jim... Jimmie.... Jamie.... Jimmy...

50. God;

No explanation necessary. It was a small appearance... indeed, a non-verbal one... which will make a fantastic cameo when the books finally become that big-budget Disney miniseries... produced, directed by, and starring Michael Sheen... sorry Rocky Flintstone. It may take a worldwide casting search to find an actor who can accurately convey the nuanced layers of wit, omniscient wisdom, and surprise at how many people showed up to Giselle and Tony's wedding. He clearly runs Heaven about as well as Sir James runs Steele's (angels have to wait for a bell-end to cum before they get their wings) and he clearly cares enough about the eternal cycle of good vs. evil to send Belinda hurtling back to Earth. What a stand-up guy. Strange that her heavenly experiences didn't lead Belinda to question her Norse beliefs, though.

Rocky's Comment;
What a great placing... at number 50... apart from 69, this must be the sweet spot for a sitting on the fence type of approval? When writing this I couldn't resist the desire to give Belinda some sort of approval on her thoughts about the church carpark from a higher authority. Stuck in her car with no one to communicate with... (she obviously couldn't get a cell signal otherwise she would have rung Chiara, still stuck in her flat) who better than God... be he of Norse origins or otherwise... I suspect they're all brothers enjoying a glass of Chardonnay at their local wine bar somewhere near the North Pole Star... but that's just me. Also having God involved in the story gives the material a sort of everlasting feeling, continuity from the past to the future no matter what Belinda may be experiencing at that moment in time. Did I hear the name "Sp00ns" whispering in the background... Amen.

49. Cedric;

It must be tough being approximately 81 years old and eternally trapped inside a magic equestrian store. Cedric has made it work by outsourcing all of the hard work to his junior staff and riding the building's ancient elevators to get his nostrils around the bosoms of attractive young women. The only price he pays is to be occasionally harvested for his moles. Not a lot to ask, really.

Rocky's Comment;

Most people over the age of 80 never get the chance to stay in the work environment because quite rightly they've been up for retirement for many years. So logically Cedric is not whom he appears at first sight. We can only conjecture that he's 55 years old and made up to look 81. But that's being a bit cynical and making his nostrils voyeurish... which indeed they might well be. I prefer to stick with the original story and admit that Cedric is the big cheese of Forsters... indeed his payslip names him as Cedric Forster and long may he control that very small and revealing lift to the ladies fitting floor.

48. Paddy the Barman;

This Northern Irish heart throb is loyal to a fault. Where would the Confidential Order of Cookware Knights be without someone to serve them cold, Australian chardonnay? Paddy also has remarkable self-control not to have been drawn into the outright pornography perpetrated in his bar every single day. It looks like we'll be spending more time in East Berlin in future books, so I'm hopeful that we'll see characters routinely travelling between the Continent and the UK, via the airport. Anything to give us more time with the Heathrow Pentra Long Bar's number one employee.

Rocky's Comment;
Paddy could well be my much younger cousin, who like me, emigrated from the Emerald Isle over 45 years ago. Competent, makes a neat cocktail for all the MI6 types frequenting the Pentra Long Bar and very tolerant of the client base his excellent service attracts. The whole Belinda Blinked scenario coupled with the Glee Team interaction is reliant on a good watering hole and I doubt if this will change in future books. Big decisions are afoot and Belinda is not one to shirk them... indeed she will be the instigator and God help Paddy when the East Germans hit town. For those of you who like to visit real places in London and why not the Pentra, it's today known as the Renaissance London Heathrow Hotel on Bath Road. At the very least have a drink in the Long Bar with your Glee Team and watch the aircraft (in my day it was Concorde) take off from next door's airport runway.
By the way, whilst Paddy has now taken up Maeve's old position as receptionist at Steeles, he's still doing the evening shift at the Pentra Long Bar... got to pay the rent somehow...

47. James Dribble;

One of the forensic accountants recruited by Sir James in *Lockdown 69*, James Dribble is, as his name suggests, yet another James. By my reckoning, that makes seven characters with James or Jim in their name, without mentioning the James *and* Jamie who host the podcast. (Is Rocky's book of baby names stuck open on the one page?) Despite his unappealing surname, Dribble is the quintessential Englishman. Charming and passionate, he passed his Japanese lead erogenous zone course with flying colours, and sure knows his way around the backseat of a Rolls Royce. Indeed, he exemplifies all the traits of that most famous British spy (also named James) which were lacking in Sp00ns. He'll have to appear in the book proper before moving any further up the rankings, but based on his performance thus far, what's not to l00ve?

Rocky's Comment;
James Dribble is another Belinda Blinked character who starts off as possibly a damp squib but when given word space starts to grow exponentially. The fact he's called James is another freak happening in the development of the series and as they say, when you lose a James as in Sp00ner, another one magically pops up albeit in Lockdown 69. Belinda, whilst getting off to a frosty start with Dribble, does admire his leather suitcase and of course when Belinda gets what she wants she feels great! This inevitably leads to further action and the rear of a specially adapted Rolls Royce seems like the right place... certainly better than the previously proposed Benny Bella's Brother's milk float.

46. Tony Sylvester;

I wish I could place Steele's Managing Director higher, and I guess he earns points for loyalty. (He deserves a few just for that scintillating brainstorm sesh around Sir James' favourite whiteboard with Belinda.) Unfortunately, despite being with us since the catalytic job interview, Tony's never quite emerged as the character he should've been. His erratic mood swings are unnerving, and enough to make anyone feel like the office cat. He missed the many neon red light signals that his brother was a backstabbing bastard. And he fell for not one but *two* double-agents. In a row. I'm remaining deeply unconvinced he's right for the job of Chairman. Here's hoping Belinda deposes Tony at series' end.

Rocky's Comment;
Yes, Tony has been a bit of a disappointment throughout the series. Unlike James Dribble, as above, he started off with a big bang at the job interview and has fizzled like a damp squib ever since... much like his love life. We have to be thankful he recruited Belinda when he did and not some other person who wouldn't have galvanised the sales team as Belinda has. Obviously, he can't be blamed for the genetics his family has given him but his choice of Giselle and Maeve as lovers and Bella as his International Sales Director shows he's beginning to lose his way. Perhaps that's what Sir James has in mind, appoint a weak character as his successor and control him from the shadows as Tony's past lovers have done. I think he's done extremely well to achieve such a high ranking position and one can only wonder where he'll be in five years' time... unemployed? or Chief Executive Monroe Corp??
Business is Brutal Tony!

45. Mimi;

This Scottish spy is ever so reliable! With her Bob haircut and trademark Woodlouse car, Mimi deserves far more credit for her initiative, preparedness, and safe driving skills. I can't help thinking that if she had joined the gang in Australia, it wouldn't have been quite the debacle it became.

Rocky's Comment;
I imagine Mimi as the archetypal "Sp00ner Girl," beautiful, seductive and with a tremendous sense of fashion… albeit in Bob haircuts and rain coats. Well… it is in Scotland (notoriously rains all the time) where she has to perform her duties at present. Perhaps as in "real showtime life" she'll step up into Sp00ners shoes when the Duchess gets round to replacing him in her spying organisation. Let's hope her surname has two "00's" in it for continuity purposes. Mmmmm…. Mimi 0'T00le???

44. Señor Zip;

One of the most delightful recurring figures of season six, Señor Zip approaches his job in a far more sensible manner than certain other spies who will remain unnamed. His gadgets are quite fun too (dobedobedo), and he's happy to splash out for the expensive gift hamper... with fresh mussels and everything! Just don't call him for backup requests; it's not his department. Thought you should know.

Rocky's Comment;
In the UK we have a fire lighter called Zip Firelighters and as it's my job to light our open fire every now and again I tend to use Zip. So, this is a small shout out to a fiery character who helps me set things alight... as Senor Zip does when he communicates with Belinda. Long may his gadgets continue to enlighten the spying world because these guys need all the help they can get! Hey Sr. Zip those ankle bracelets haven't done so well... but I'd just love one of those garment cutting lasers!

43. Ken Dewsbury;

What a fucking loon. The chapter in Big Ken's cellar is the single grimmest piece of writing in Rocky's *oeuvre*. The voyeuristic RSM from God's own country clearly needs to invest in some more state-of-the-art equipment; anything without multi-coloured wires stapled to the wall would be an improvement! Yet I admire someone who knows what they want. And somehow, aside from the occasional mislaid shipment of couscous evaporators and some invoices so wrong they're doing Big Titties Matilda's head in, it seems to be working out for him.

Rocky's Comment;
The first Xmas special, for me, characterises the true Ken Dewsbury. The way he slides a grubby envelope, with a no doubt much used Christmas card inside, across the table towards Belinda and then almost grudgingly thanks her for his best sales year ever. Classic salesman attitude... and I've worked with lots of them. Another telling moment is when Ken drives Belinda to his grimy cellar flat just outside the centre of Leeds. This is based on real fact as Wilma and I lived above it for at least one glorious year, saving up to buy our first house. But what I really like about Ken Dewsbury is his unabashed pride in telling Belinda that the nearly derelict property has been in his family for over 100 years. It's so telling that Ken doesn't stop to think that perhaps he should do a bit of building work to the property and make something better of it. Salt of the earth... a Yorkshire man... if it's not broke, don't fix it... But Ken, you do need to repair it from time to time. So, you can imagine Wilma and I's excitement when Jamie tells us he's moving into a student house just around the corner from where we subsisted all those years ago.... and yes... that empty basement flat is still there! Need a short term rental in Leeds, UK anyone?

42. Grigor Calanski;

With a dismissive attitude toward women, and an inability to find the asshole, this bear-like Russian entrepreneur is a sleaze of the highest order. Grigor hasn't yet endeared himself to me, but this caviar expert has given Belinda access to one of the biggest continents yet... yes that's right, the continent of Russia. We don't know what happened to the Soviet Union in Rocky's world after that glorious Wall came down. Perhaps with Belinda transferring to East Germany, the Soviet swine will come into greater prominence?

Rocky's Comment;
Grigor is a hard guy to get to know, believe me I've tried but I just can't drink vodka. A classic no hoper who's made good, starting out as the son of a Kulak peasant family and making a big success of himself. But he's a big fan of Belinda and that has to be a good thing. Now with her new duties Belinda might decide she needs to spend more time in the USSR. No one can avoid doing business with over 200,000,000 people and Belinda's too savvy to ignore them... they need her and her pots and pans!!! Grigor in his own ebullient way will push his caviar and cigar corporation into the pots and pans ecosystem and no doubt make a killing. As long as it's not at Belinda's expense... who cares? Business is Brutal Calanski.

41. Contessa Luccia Lorenzo;

Who will ever forget this aristocrat having smoke literally blown up her ass? Sp00ns assured us that she'd recover after he stunned her to stone and took 17 minutes from her life at the airport. But given how well the rest of his espionage practices worked out, I suspect we may have said "Ciao" to this particular royal.

Rocky's Comment;
Contessa Luccia Lorenzo is very well connected in the Italian aristocracy and is an acolyte of Belinda. A school girl friend of Aldo Fellini, Luccia holds the key to bringing his supermarket chain on board. But we have to ask... which way will he swing... Belinda or Steeles Pots and Pans. I suppose it'll depend on whose got his balls in their hands... with Belinda around I suspect she'll be the winner who'll take it all and leave Bella crying with her "Cry no More" utility knife for comfort. As for "Ciao," I'd rather say "Arrivederci"! But hey wait... did we mean it the other way round???

40. Clarence, Duke of Epsom;

Horny since birth, Clarence feels like he should be super-important to the overall plot, married as he is to the head of British Intelligence, and routinely hobnobbing with Sir James, Chiara, and other notables. Yet ever since we learned about that time he scrambled around on the floor at Claridge's, desperately trying to scoop up his wife's love eggs which had broken free of their moorings due to excess lube, his reputation has been irrevocably smeared. (Also, his idea of a good time is taking Bella of all people to look at some old family portraits. What a hag.)

Rocky's Comment;
Sir James Godwin's golf partner, and for all we know his partner in "crime", the Duke of Epsom is an unfortunate leech on society. He's a big Port drinker, loves Chicken Kiev in garlic sauce and ogling young lady's bodies with a piece of lipstick hidden in his rear…. we'll leave that thought there. However, his entanglement with Bella at the Tombola didn't turn out as he'd wished and his Duchess wife, the head of MI6, taught him a salutary lesson. Never again did Clarence stray… and it's good to know that his wife didn't share her morals too widely, potentially stopping any involvement with Belinda and the Duchess's other female friends.

39. Cristina Rouse;

Peter Rouse's wife.
Sir James' niece.
An internal spy.
An unusually intense interest in office microwaves.
And… at least in a parallel timeline… infertile but with a knack for cute kitsch accessories.
I fully expect the spunky Cristina to come into prominence in upcoming books. For now, let's all remember the quintessential moment when she draped her tits over Belinda's ass. I've tried her method of greeting prospective lovers… strangely it doesn't seem to work for me.

Rocky's Comment;
Finding a microwave that "does fish" was one of Cristina's major discoveries when she visited the Steeles offices that fateful day in late December. It was a blow that Peter could never recover from in his own lifetime. As the mulled wine slipped gaily down his throat, he knew that every office in his own organisation would have one installed by the new year. Yes, Cristina had nabbed the budget reserved for a new lift and the old one would have to muddle on for a while longer. However, I do think Cristina was very happy to keep things as they were. You see as any decent spy would tell you any opportunity to quiz a new visitor to your offices in a broken down lift would be most welcome… you never know where it might lead. Besides a precedent has been set by Jethro in NCIS… all his best interrogations take place in this highly unusual situation. Learn from the best as Cristina no doubt has. One thing I am waiting for is Jethros' ass on network TV…
Sammy, a bit of advice on your saying hello to prospective lovers… you need to have certain female attributes to use that technique, OK?

38. Alfonse Stirbacker;

The Belgian, with 300 outlets throughout the low countries, made a striking first appearance in the maze but, in future chapters, gave off the slight whiff of being a loser. All the same, if there's a kinky event taking place, he's guaranteed to be there. Whether it's a handcuffed woman caked in mud or a library sex party, a leaked security video on U Tube or a chocolate fountain (literally), Alfonse will sniff it out.

Rocky's Comment;

Alfonse is an up market sophisticated type of guy who's going through a final breakup with his much younger wife of 20 years... No wonder he gets himself invited to all the sexy parties in Brussels. He's also a successful entrepreneur and a very good catch for all those divorced ladies out there. I always thought he'd have a bit of a thing with Madam Chocolat... but her very brief liaison with Belinda may well have snuffed that one dead. Still, there's plenty to go at... Contessa Lucia being one... perhaps Monsieur Rideaux's wife fancies a change from the Belgian Colonies...

37. Ian Snail;

Steele's Head of Marketing, and part-time office radio host, became an instant classic after his first (and thus far only) appearance in the season six finale. He's apparently a prude but didn't seem so during the climactic 24-hour bonking party. (Thank goodness Bella finally got the chance to cross him off her colleague bingo list!) For someone who's so judgemental about his co-workers, though, I have a few questions.
1) As Head of Marketing, where was he when the conference organisers were looking for companies to promote at the Millennium Dome Building?
2) Why didn't he use the concept of product placement, before Belinda found out about it from telly?
3) Why did Belinda have to invent a frying pan named Sam to encourage small children into the kitchen?
I hope we hear more from Ian's radio gig (Snail's Mail, as the podcast has titled it), if only because he will no doubt be a sarcastic commentator on the story at hand. Anything to encourage the people at Steele's to take a good, long look at themselves.

Rocky's Comment;
Iain as I really meant to write because with the addition of an S you get Snail... OK you've gotta twist the first I into an L... but you get the idea... and yes it doesn't work, so I hate him. He's the sort of greasy marketing type who always steals the salesman's ideas and turns them into a marketing initiative which he claims the success of for himself... yes... I'm bitter... because I've been that salesman... But let's get to the questions...
Any growing organisation will pick up people and job positions as it develops... Steeles is no exception and because of the tumultuous success Belinda brought to the company, Tony was able to add a Marketing Manager to the team. Hence Iain Snail... When he was appointed, I'll leave to your imagination.
Question 2 has the same answer as #1, he wasn't around... I also doubt he understands the concept... (I have to stop being bitter).

Small children and kitchens should never be in the same sentence never mind place so let's disown that comment immediately. Have you read my book on Sweet Treats?

Etsy signed by myself

https://www.etsy.com/uk/listing/1051458647/

Amazon UK https://amzn.to/3QilHYE

Amazon USA https://amzn.to/3SlJgCJ

Now that's real cooking for kids... grown up or small.

So in conclusion if Iain Snail wants to progress in Steeles Pots and Pans he'd better start being nice to me.

Fuck off Iain.

36. Hans and Greta Schweinsteiger;

I have several questions about Jamie's accent work throughout the books. Rarely do the questions loom as large as when thinking of Greta Schweinsteiger, who treads the delicate line between cartoon squirrel and psychopath. Hans and Greta appear to be stuck in a fairy tale, and I haven't quite figured out how exactly their business model with Price Keen and Bargain Store works, but gosh, Greta knows how to pleasure our title character. Some of the credit must go to her crate full of dildos from New Guinea for sure. Will Belinda ever return to the haunted warehouse to complete her sibling double? Stay tuned to find out!

Rocky's Comment;
I really do think these two identical but fundamentally different characters should have made their own ranking, so I'll do it now.
36a Greta Schweinsteiger
36b Hans Schweinsteiger
I've put Greta before Hans as I know she'd insist on it being that way, but also, she's had a lot more plot to date than Hans. They both reappear in Lockdown 69 where Hans pulls his weight as much as Greta, but that visit by Des and Belinda to their warehouse confirms my choice. Whilst the boys go off and do man things with stock and stuff, the girls get down to it in the warm comfy office trying out new underwear and of course assessing New Guinea sourced dildos. What else would we expect of Belinda, never mind Bella and Giselle... now she's back to being a team player. Of course, I hear all the hard-bitten sales guys out there shouting... "It's what management does... the Boss stays in the office whilst we do the work on the shop floor."
I guess the Andy Milston story bears that point out once again. On reflection I don't think I've ever met a hard-bitten sales gal, but I suppose there's still time? Could Greta be one?

35. D'Artagnan Raspberry;

D'Artagnan, or "Arty" to his friends, is known at Steele's as "Mr No-One," the head accountant who raises no eyebrows. Yet, as we learned in *Lockdown 69*, he was actually a criminal mastermind, who ended up soaring high above his useless co-conspirators, going as far as to subconsciously convince a CIA mole that he deserved to live. For his name alone, Arty earns some plaudits, but he's also blessed with quick thinking and enough rudimentary medical knowledge to patch up a bullet wound with some toilet paper. Sadly, for him, Arty didn't end up getting away with his fortune, yet further proof that in Rocky's unimpeachable moral calculus, cheaters never prosper.

Rocky's Comment;

I was immensely pleased, (as I was immensely distraught at Iain Snails ranking), that D'Artagnan Raspberry made it to #35. In the world of Pop he's in the top 40!! But what a character, if you thought Bisch was naughty then Arty will lead you to the Devil's door. Apart from being a mathematical genius and ex special ops, he's also a snappy dresser with a toned body to die for. He's for sure a male Belinda... with many of her traits. Not for no reason was he known at Steeles as "Mr No One" and as we all know, Belinda herself doesn't say much... instead, like Mr Raspberry, she listens and takes it all in. As they say, it's the quiet ones you have to watch.

But, Sir James and Tony, how much more do you have to learn about running an international business when your head accountant turns out to be the biggest villain of them all. Arty has more to do, and next time he mightn't play so gently... beware...

34. Aunty Bobbi, Uncle Ariel, and their baby rottweiler Fizzfudge;

Bella's relatives are the family I always wanted but never knew I needed. There's a real "70's dinner party" vibe about them that makes me all warm and fuzzy. I just want to join the fam as they forage for mushrooms by day and attend an avant-garde interpretation of Chekhov by night before heading home for some late-night vegan snacks and a good climate change documentary.

Rocky's Comment;
What utter nonsense this is... a dog ranking #34. Just wait until we get to Toffee Apple Chew I hear you all gasp. Well to be honest, this ranking can't be because of the rest of that absolute rabble. Bella, where did you come from? But saying all that, family is family... "yes family" and we should never forget it. Who knows what terrible plight Bella and Belinda may get into where they need a baby rottweiler called "Fizzfudge" to extract them. Besides add Bobbi to Bella and Belinda and what do you get? Of course, the 3B's. To develop that just a little bit further, add Benny, Bella and Bobbi Ridley and you could say, "they was robbed".

33. Bill from HR;

I'm largely trolling Alice by putting this piece of cardboard-flavoured nothing in my top third. Yet Bill's very absence from the text is what makes him so remarkable. Rocky has brilliantly crafted this lacuna at the centre of Steele's, symbolising the emptiness of the modern-day corporate world, and the chilling effect which bureaucracy can cast over our natural ways of co-existence. Revealed in the book's very first chapter as someone for whom sex is not his "responsibility", Bill stands at the opposite end of the spectrum from Belinda. More so even than Bisch, who represents the horror of how easily good can turn to evil, the HR manager embodies something far more harrowing: a failure to recognise the eternal human truth that one can't find noble, loyal, sexually devastating people purely through bland recruitment procedures. No, one must instead seek them out in the real world: in second-rate drama schools and country inns, at authentic family Christmas gatherings and backstage at the O2. Bill is a triumphant satire of the zeitgeist, and I remain hopeful he will enter into the climax. So, to speak.

Rocky's Comment;

Well... that was a timely piece of writing Sammy. Well done, a classic bit of clap trap added to a character who is a complete nonentity and was only at the first interview because of his position in the organisation. Bill is the typical company employee, so absorbed in his own day to day job that he can't see the big picture. But Human Resources is a bit like that, dealing with people every day does that to an employee and Bill is lack lustre at best. As we all know you can't have an organisation like Steeles where everyone shines, you need the dumbos to balance the team and oh boy Bill sure is a dumbo. A perpetual paper pusher, Bill doesn't exist, he subsists and that's one of the reasons he doesn't get invited to the Pentra with the big girls. It's also certain that he's no favourite of the Glee Team and his small cameo in the COCK conference room in Lockdown 69 will certainly put him in Sir James Godwin's bad books. It's no coincidence that he wasn't involved in the hiring of IT support guy James Sp00ner, or at the brain storming, now known as "thought showering", session at Sir James ancestral home when Tony and Belinda deduced the source of their newly discovered problems. Yes, Bill is a necessary fixture in the organisation, but he'll never become the icon that Jim Thompson truly is.

32. Countess Zara of Leningrad;

Running an upscale brothel can be a nightmare in this heavily unionised, rule-bound age. (It was one of the less-reported causes of Brexit.) Zara, as we learned at the wedding, is unfortunately rather backward in her views on people with disability. Yet the fiery Russian, with the grace of a ballerina and a rapacious sexual appetite, was the first to clock that Maeve had something to offer besides a good phone manner. And she kindly manned the phones(!) at Steele's while the rest of COCK took an urgent meeting in *Lockdown 69*. So, she can't be all bad.

Rocky's Comment;
Unlike Grigor Calanski the Countess of Leningrad is much liked amongst fans, perhaps it's her undying love for Sir James, though I suspect that might be more of a gold digger situation. Whatever, she seems to have given up on her Amsterdam based operation in favour of Steeles Pots and Pans. I hope the thinnish man is keeping her profits rolling in and that all the girls she employs are being well looked after. Another toughie, just like the Duchess, Belinda seems to attract this type of hands-on lady. No doubt she will assist in the development of pots and pans sales in mother Russia, or as Zara would know it, the CCCP... which stands for Союз Советских Социалистических Республик. The Union of Soviet Socialist Republics if you didn't know... or perhaps we'll just move on...
Long live the Ukraine.
No pots and pans sales to Russia!!
Belinda does not break embargoes!!

31. Old Mother Blumenthal;

One of Jamie's more successful adventures in accent work, Old Mother Blumenthal's burlesque career may only have been OK but she spends most of her time getting absolutely sloshed and improvising torch ballads in the Garden of England (The county of Kent). Who can fault it?

Rocky's Comment;
Belinda's mother is a complex character about whom we know very little. With a German background, she unusually kept her own maiden name of Blumenthal when she married her husband Bobby. Or Robert as he's officially known. A stepsister to the infamous East German industrial magnate Wolfgang Bisch (not generally known) she may well be in a position to do very well when he dies. Belinda of course as her daughter would also be well placed, and as we now know actually takes over the day to day operations of the group. Her penchant for a glass of wine, much like my own, does lead her down a path of delightful abandonment of her wifely duties and it seems Bobby had as much a hand in the rearing of the young Belinda as her mother. Unfortunately, whilst wine fine tunes my writing, no such accolade can be attributed to Mrs Blumenthal's hobby of singing. In her younger day she was something of a singer, being a member of some famous youth choirs, which then lead to a couple of recording contracts with Deutsch Gramophone. However, nothing much came of it and soon she was whisked off to Kent in South East England to marry Bobby Brown and become a singing housewife.

30. Peter Rouse;

The Netherlands' answer to Steve Jobs, Peter Rouse veered between being Belinda's (married) soul mate and just really bloody weird. (Surely anyone sane would have taken Belinda to hospital after her meltdown at the Restaurant d'Albert.) In recent years, however, he has disappeared from the scene entirely. I like to think that Peter represented Belinda's naïveté, back when she thought that working in pots and pans was just a way to meet handsome men who shared her sense of, uh, humour. Before long, our heroine would discover that the industry was actually one of the most important barriers standing between a world of truth and justice, and one of organised crime and total anarchy. Peter never became what he should have, but I look forward to Rocky's explanation for his magic powers, allowing him to put someone in thrall to him by the use of his semen. Did he pluck an enchanted dildo from a stone when he was a boy?

Rocky's Comment;
Peter A Rouse is a dedicated husband to his wife Cristina. After his encounter with Belinda at the Tombola, and her subsequent visit to the Amsterdamm offices, he decided to settle down and concentrate on having a family. As we found out in a Xmas Special, things weren't going too well in that direction. With the mysterious overnight loss of his purchasing Director Pieter Robbins whilst on a buying trip to East Berlin, Peter has also had to help out in the purchasing department. He's a busy guy and with the development of his stores outside of Holland, he doesn't get much time to chase the likes of Belinda. The old mud runes he drew on her naked body back in the maze have also well and truly dried out, and in order to impose his sexual will on her once more, he'll have to get down and dirty. The question is, will Cristina let him do it, or will she too become involved in a never ending triad of sexual mud slinging.

29. Cosmo Macaroon;

As an Australian, I can't claim that Rocky's portrayal of the country, or Jamie's voices, are especially authentic. I can, however, attest that Cosmo is a gem of a character. Gifted (albeit in a haphazard way) with cookery sills, Cosmo handles multiple TV gigs with ease while also keeping a close eye on his fan club mailing list. What's more, unlike his agent Cornelius, Cosmo knows a good deal when he sees it. What he doesn't know is a giant crane cam in his dressing room when he sees it, but hey, nobody's perfect.

Rocky's Comment;
I was fortunate to be able to spend some time after the last Australian Tour travelling around Eastern Australia. Sammy... scrub and dust... dust and scrub was all I could see. My research for the book proved to be impeccable and was totally confirmed when I travelled from Sydney to Adelaide by train on the Indian Pacific. A glorious experience and the Chardonnay flowed non-stop! Early one morning we stopped at Broken Hill and as the sun came up all I could see for miles and miles was scrub... combined with a very fine dust. No proper rain for over 30 years made these conditions ideal for the outback. Thank goodness for old radios and Flying Doctors. Cosmo of course never gets to the outback but he should consider an outside cooking series for all the suburban townies living in Oz's big cities. Bella would be inundated with fan club requests and Cosmo would enhance his career as well as his new pots and pans supplier Steeles. I do wonder how that will work out now Belinda is in charge of Bisch... or can Bella retain the account as well as Cosmo's fan base.

28. Professor Slinz;

Devoting his life to market-smashing cookware meant that Slinz died a virgin... depending on how you define "spending your final moments on Earth being waterboarded by a crazed woman's vagina". Discovered as a humble cauldron-maker on the streets of Hanover, Slinz emigrated to the British Isles where he was responsible for the world-beating Tri-Oxy-Brillo range and perhaps also the Cry-No-More knife which... so far hasn't exactly taken off. (They can't all be winners.) When he wasn't hunched over blueprints, Slinz was capable of giving an exhaustive (and exhausting) tour of the Scottish factory too. Tragically, this genius was the first death to take place in *Belinda Blinked*. Gone too soon, the Prof-Prof with the half-moon specs was denied a state funeral, perhaps a victim of the British Royal Family's reluctance to publicise their long-standing connection to Germany? One can only speculate. Regardless, he will be mourned by many.

Rocky's Comment;
Professor Slinz's death is meant to be a timely warning to all those readers who try out everything described in these books. Once again please do not waterboard with your vaginal lids, it can not only lead to friction burns, but you could suffocate your partner. However, whilst the Prof was still alive and working in his laboratory he made some very interesting discoveries. Here's one scene which never made the books but highlights the dedication inventors all over the world exhibit.

A visit to the Laboratory;
Belinda knocked on the big wooden door and looked at Bella and Giselle. 'This should be fun....'
'Zenter.'
She opened the door and they walked into a large laboratory. Belinda could see pots and pans scattered all over various benches. A white coated, grey bearded gent was busily turning on jets of flame and burning out their centres. He stopped and turned round to greet the Glee Team.
'Gud mornink Miss Blumenthal, I see you 'aff arrived with your two delicious companions for the first guided tour of our vonderful factory. Now, to be honest we ave worked very ard to prepare for you! But I ave a question about the stories I have eard of YOU and your Glee Team!

Belinda stepped back in amazement; she was surprised that the Glee Team's fame had gone before them... but surely this old gent couldn't be interested in sex?

'Now strip off please, I vant you naked immediately.'
Belinda looked at Giselle, who looked at Bella and Belinda did as she was told. She took off her high heels and placed them on a nearby bench, then her jacket and skirt.
'No, no, no, don't place them zere, zey vill get destroyed... use zat elegant coat stand.'
Professor Slinz pointed to a corner of the room and Belinda hung her garments on it. She continued without another word removing her white silk blouse. Dressed skimpily in her thong and brassiere she unclasped the bra and let her magnificent breasts entice the Professors eyes away from a saucepan he was burning the centre out of. He immediately lost his aim and scorched the plastic handle which went up in a puff of smoke. He glanced back at the damaged utensil and said,
'Very interesting... I fink we haf defined a new test.'
He smiled at Belinda who was now removing her thong. She hung it up with the rest of her clothing and tiptoed naked back to join the girls and the Professor at the testing benches.

The Professor put down the pot he was scrutinising with a large magnifying glass and rubbed Belinda's bare ass with his free hand.
'Superb contours, my darlink.' he breathed. Belinda waggled her breasts at him and he sighed,
'Ze zings I do for zis company.'
Slinz took Belinda's breasts in his two hands and felt their unfettered weight.
'Hmmm... about two kilos each.' He let them go brushing the engorging nipples briefly and making a note in his laboratory manual.
'Excellent!'
Belinda was pleased whilst listening to Giselle and Bella sniggering in the background.

'Now you may tink I vas a little bit forward in feelink your titties dear Belinda, but zere is good scientific reasoning behind zis.' He once again rubbed Belinda's ass.
'In my studies I have discovered that the ideal weight of a pan or pot should be exactly the weight of the female breast using them.'

Belinda Blinked;

She thought, if true this information was of earth shattering importance.
Utensil weight labelling throughout the world would change overnight.
Would we use the brassiere cup size or do as the Professor had just done,
feel the weight of one tit and then the pan? Would future department
stores have curtain covered tit holding areas... Belinda's mind came back
to the present. Out of the corner of her eye she could see Giselle and
Bella assessing the weight of each other's breasts....

The Professor had selected two pots from the new Steele's Oxy Brillo
range. He held them out to Belinda and asked her to hold them, one in
each hand.
'Now, wave each pot in turn up and down and all around.' he instructed
her.
Belinda did so.
The Professor videotaped the actions and prepared it for replaying back
onto a large screen at the bottom of the lab.
'I vill now show you the naked truth Belinda and highlight the shocking
damage our industry iz doing to its end users and what we propose to do
to rectify zis disgraceful situation!'

Belinda watched on in horror as the tape played. Surely her bare tits
weren't that saggy... but wait a minute, what the hell was wrong with the
left one... it looked deformed compared to her right.
The Professor noted with satisfaction her annoyance.
'Belinda, do you 'ave a problem?'
'Yes Professor, I do, why is my left tit looking so deformed compared to
the right tit?'
'Ha Ha, you ave spotted it immediately, it iz because your left boob is out
of balance with the pot your left hand iz holding.... just look again at the
right boob, it iz performing perfectly because it iz in harmony with ze pot!'
Belinda was amazed, you had to hand it to these boffins, they thought of
everything.

'Now to conclusively prove to you that vat I am saying iz ze truth we vill
repeat the procedure but this time your left tit will be perfect whilst your
right tit vill be deformed.'
Belinda repeated the exercise as the Professor filmed, but this time he
kept the camera rolling.

'Now, Giselle and Bella please strip also. Hand me the perfect pan for your breast veights and I vill discuss a new theory I ave on ze handles.'

Belinda Blinked;

Yes, Professor Slinz will be sorely missed.

27. Chiara Montague;

With a name like that, Chiara didn't have to do much work to find herself in the top third of the competition. Yet she's certainly earned her place: intimately acquainted with the aristocracy, a keen skier, an avowed anti-racist, and happy to use her infamous sewing skills to protect Great Britain's business secrets. An oft unsung heroine who may still be trapped in Belinda's loft apartment. I'm hoping the parrot food holds out. #freechiara

Rocky's Comment;

One of the newish glamour girls of the series, Chiara will always be the posho who never quite makes the spotlight. On the edge of the Glee Team, missing out on the trip to the Costa del Sol in Hazels newspaper financed aeroplane, meant she never really made it. The fact everyone seems to think she's still locked in Belinda's central London penthouse makes no sense to me. Of course she's got her own key... and she's allowed to park her Aston Martin in Belinda's very large garage any time she wants. Having a free parking spot like that in central London would make me want to be friends. Yes, we all have high hopes for Chiara and what with Belinda's new responsibilities, she may well be one of the first to cross the Anglo German divide.

26. Petra;

Oh my God, Jamie. Petra has earned a legion of fans in spite of, or because of, her borderline incomprehensible warblings. Although she's linked in our minds with Herr Bisch, the books have never explicitly stated that she was involved in his odious schemes. If the melodious East German is redeemed in future volumes, I'll move her further up the ranking. Until then, I höpe you understaand.

Rocky's Comment;
Petra's time as Bisch's personal assistant must indicate that she knew most of what he got up to. The office meeting with Sp00ner and Smiffy... aka Belinda undercover, showed us that she was closely allied to him. It was Sp00n's seduction techniques which paved the way for the discovery of the evidence trail leading to Giselle as the Special One. By diverting Petra's attention he allowed Smiffy the opportunity to find the one crucial document. Later at Bisch's Schloss everything becomes even more sinister as Petra has the security cameras follow our two intrepid spies around the building. Is Petra a double timing Bisch employee, waiting for Belinda to make a fatal error, or is she just in need of a decent job? Only time and Belinda Blinked Book 7 will tell.

25. Wayne Burt, aka Dr. Pieter Robbins;

A weird freaking dude. It's comforting to realise that Dr Robbins' lunatic performance in Amsterdam was just that: a performance. What we took for a manic, scissors-wielding, cackling voyeur was in truth a plain-speaking huckster from the streets of Philly who had four million cans of baked beans, a travelling desk, and a grand plan. A veteran of the US Army of the Rhine... that famed unit who saw much action during the, er, Cold War... Wayne Burt was a man of vision, with no qualms about getting his head tattooed, all in the name of making his fortune. And he would have got away with it, if it wasn't for those meddling COCKs.

Rocky's Comment;
I cannot believe any reader didn't see through the Dr Robbins act from the very start. It was obvious from the word go that he was a nutcase... and they make the best sort of villains. What is of greater interest, is why did Bisch place Wayne Burt in the Rouse Supermarket chain's offices. Obviously as a former Quarter Master in the US Army he would be well used to purchasing foodstuffs, so as a purchasing Director he was well hidden. However surely Belinda wasn't the first supplier whom he took his quirky sexual desires out on? Didn't Cristina Rouse in her internal role as company intelligence officer know of his dark side? I'm sure Rouse Supermarkets purchased stuff from Bisch, so there would have been a natural contact there, but how did Burt, aka Dr Robbins get appointed? Does Peter Rouse owe Bisch a favour, money, or the property on which lots of his shops are built? So many questions. It's all to play for and remember Helga is still in place waiting for her new boss to walk through the office door and seduce her on that heavily stained leather covered desk. I do have to ask if she'll send back an FBI report immediately, or will the wily Helga wait 3 or 4 years building up her evidence base as she did on her last case. And speaking of her last case, here's how she interviewed for the job...

Dr Pieter Robbins...
Interviewing the new assistant;

The good Doctor paced his room intensely. He was thinking, he was thinking very hard. Whilst disappointment never took him by surprise, he was frankly troubled by the day's proceedings. You see Dr Pieter Robbins was interviewing for a new personal assistant. To date he'd interviewed 5 candidates… two of which were men, which made him feel very important… he'd never had a man working for him before. It was novel he thought… perhaps too novel for him, a dyed in the wool though recently appointed and hopefully upstanding senior manager in Peter Rouse's organisation. But… reluctantly they didn't feel right for him… so over lunch he'd decided that the three females were also no better than the two males, which meant he had one candidate left.

The knock at his office door brought him back to reality….
'Come in, come in!' he half shouted.
'Dank u mijnheer Dokter.'
The last candidate sat down on a chair which was positioned to have the possibility of the late afternoon sun shining on it. Presently it was cloudy, but Pieter Robbins had hope. He ruffled through the pile of resume's trying desperately to find the relevant one. It was at the bottom of the pile as it should have been. His left foot began tapping, music started to play in his head, he put his left hand on his knee and applied some pressure. It all stopped.
'Good,' he thought, 'I am in control of this situation.'

'I see you have had much experience with various organisations, has any of this been in a purchasing role?'
The candidate nodded vigorously and said,
'Ja mijnheer Dokter.' in an enthusiastic way.
Dr Robbins smiled and rubbed his hands. This was indeed a good start, and even better the sun was starting to shine.
'Forgive me, but is the sunshine bothering you?'
'Ja, een beetje meneer Dokter.'
'Would you like to remove your jacket, before we continue… I always like my staff to be comfortable in their place of work.'

Dr Robbins smiled, got up and took the denim jacket. He hung it happily on an old wooden coat stand which he'd inherited with the job just a few months ago. The music started to play in his head again, but not as loudly…
"shooting stars never stop…"

He quickly shook his head and continued...

'Now, where were we... ah, yes, we have ascertained you have suitable prowess for working with me in purchasing matters. As you will already know, it is a matter of producing and copying contracts with our suppliers. Can I confirm you are familiar with this work?'
The candidate again nodded vigorously and replied,
'Mijn werk bij de Amerikaanse ambassade meneer Doctor.... was very the same...'
Robbins was no fool and he knew when he'd spotted a talent that perhaps the candidate was trying to hide from him so he quickly replied,
'Ahh... I see you speak some English... that will be very useful in this role. We have many British and American suppliers, this is very good... I am seeing you as an asset... not just an employee!'
He clapped his knee and started to hum in tune to the music in his head, this candidate was looking very promising he enthused gaily.

The candidate smiled and surreptitiously opened a couple of her white silk blouse buttons...it was getting hot now the sun was shining brightly. Dr Robbins looked on with interest, the physique was good, if not a little flabby, strong powerful legs always attracted him to a person... and the correct shoes were a must. He liked black in a shoe colour, but never white socks... no, white socks were a turn off... both male and female he thought. But all he saw this afternoon was good, this candidate was looking more promising with each passing second... and the purple socks were a definite turn on.

'I always like my assistants to dress down when they are working with me... no flashy garments, just drab smocks... flat well polished shoes... you know the score I'm sure.'
The candidate nodded and added in broken English,
'I am appy to vear vat I am told meneer Dokter.'
Robbins smiled, hummed the returning music to himself whilst letting his right knee tap and said...
'Then dear candidate I suggest grey woollen garments, all over and the position is yours...'

Agent Helga Blinked;

24. Sam the Youngish Man[ager];

Another character who was more relevant to the series in its earlier years, Sam was the first character to be described with Rocky's trademark "ish". In both of his performances, first at the Horse and Jockey and later at the Ritz (as we know, the only place to get a drink in Greater London), where he made the fatal error of having turkey in the vicinity. Still, on both occasions he managed to give Belinda the "room service" she so desperately needed. And that is what makes The Youngish Man so memorable. For the first time since she began her Steele's journey, Belinda was able to focus on pleasure for its own sake, rather than shagging for the business. A youngish, generous lover who valued her for no other reason than the intimacy of two strangers, albeit in a borderline inappropriate scenario, getting it on. And you can't doubt his work ethic: no wonder he climbed the career ladder after working both the day and night shift at his first job. (Now, can someone please clean that Stainless Steel Work Preparation Area?)

Rocky's Comment;

Sam is a lovely fella and a great sexy night in for Belinda. A man of few words who knows how to get the job done without overstaying his welcome. I have no doubt that with his catering skills Belinda will have him on the pay role at Burts Baked Beans in a very senior position. Let's be honest he couldn't make much more of a hash (beans and hash... do you like the Segway?) of it than Mr Wayne Burt himself. The true entrepreneur that Ms Blumenthal is, knows that the ailing fast bean take away chain needs a major makeover and a widening of its offering. Beans, Hash and Chicken sounds good to me, and as we all know how keen Sam is on Turkey, it may well be Beans, Hash and Turkey. It will also be interesting to see how the romantic dynamic might change when Belinda eventually becomes his boss. Will he follow the fate of the Regional Sales Managers and become relegated to the role of just another minor sexual employee as Des Martin, Ken Dewsbury and Patrick O'Hamlin seem to have become. Or will Sam strike out and seduce Belinda with, say, prawn sandwiches and prosecco? Whatever he does we can be sure that Sam the Youngish Manager will be steadily progressing his career until he reaches the zenith of the hospitality industry.

23. Hank Skank;

Hank, Jim Stirling's Chief Executive, worked his way up from student janitor to a high-flyer, hobnobbing with Ron and Nancy and enjoying his great seats at the Krankies. He's the star of one of my favourite chapters as Belinda gets her baps out in an Italian Trattoria, and Hank takes some sausage home for dessert. And he's characterised by one of Jamie's less offensive accents. He really is a rare breed.

Rocky's Comment;

Hank Skank is a fun character to write. The steel behind the bonhomie of Jim Stirling, the man who gets things done, a lover of Italian food with a European birth heritage and yet happily ensconced in beautiful, low taxes, Texas. Yes, deep down Hank is one hell of a complicated character. Truth be fair, we've not seen all that much of him to date, but he's like a volcano, rumbling away deep down in the bowels of the earth waiting for his own personal explosion of dubious sausage recipes. A man who likes "Steak, Ass and Tits," he's the sort of Chief Executive Belinda needs to find if she's going to run her newly acquired businesses with any form of success. Head and shoulders above any of the RSM's Belinda used to work with, it will be a struggle to find a similarly gifted individual based in Europe. But knowing Belinda, I'm sure the job interviews will be fun.

22. Penelope Pollet;

I suspect Chiara Montague's half-sister PP is not all that memorable to the average listener, but... I tell you this in a whisper only you can hear... something really clicked in me since her first appearance.
"No, no, no, you simple bitch!"
This might be the *MDWAP* quote I say most often in my everyday life. If you see a striking woman in a pink linen suit with orange seaming on the streets of gay Paree, invite her out for a drink, let her take her viewing stool, and see where the night takes you. Trust me.

Rocky's Comment;
Penelope Pollet is another one of the Duchess's acolytes and we're not sure whether she holds a similar role to the Duchess, at MI6, with Interpol, based in Paris. Slightly more of her character is revealed in Lockdown 69 when she offers to help Belinda with a cash injection. Being smart as Belinda is, a quick discussion with the Duchess lead onto a good business decision. We don't really know if PP is an admirer or a devious competitor of Belinda and what she does... especially in her new role at Bisch. Certainly, in PP's day job at FiveCarre she has purchased some Steeles products, but she seems to be holding off for something more. FiveCarre are capable of much bigger orders, so what's going on? Is all the air kissing and the "Oh la la's" just acting or does this crazy French bitch have a different agenda to what she's letting on? Of course, everything will be revealed, but it may just be in Belinda Blinked 11... perhaps 12? Yes, I'm still writin....

21. The Goons;

They are all gone now, the old familiar goons. Every one of them dead as are the lost kings of England. What will Bisch Herstellung do without them? They were loyal, stupid, inconsistently voiced, and blessed with poor impulse control. Basically a bunch of Bellas. Maybe Bisch will be better off, after all.

Rocky's Comment;
Sammy… The Goons at number 21… are you stark raving mad?? This ranking reminds me of a stupid Christmas pop song making number 1 in mid December. It should not be there!! And neither should these guys… besides being incompetent, they're also terrorists… two words which do not sit happily beside each other. Also, there's no way you're going to associate my dear lovely Bella with these numpkins… she's far too good for that insult. Why you'll soon be lumping the magnificent James Sp00ner in with them if we're not careful. Poppycock… what a load of drivel… Sammy, this is virtually the top 20… say you won't do this again… promise? OK then you're forgiven… just…

20. Gerramima St Frostfurst;

This Liverpudlian acting mistress at RADS (that's the Royal Academy of Drama and Stuff if you've been too scared to visit Liverpool) is one of my most treasured one-off characters. Having spent several years at drama school myself, let me tell you that Rocky's trademark research really paid off here. You can spare yourself the expense of those fancy schools where Stanley Tucci and Dame Helen wasted their youths. Gerramima got it right first time:

"Acting is the art of pretending to be someone you're not actually the person of."

It's a shame that her heart sank without trace after Belinda's award-worthy performance. But the role of the frilly-lidded former chorus dancer would still be ideal for someone of the calibre of Dame Judi. Or, really, any of Jamie's favourite dames.

Rocky's Comment;

Gerramima, or Gerry for short, yeah that's what they do in the North of England... shorten your name to virtually nothing, or is it because they, quite rightly in my opinion, can't spell the name. So, Gerry is actually based on a real person, a very real live person who thankfully hasn't cottoned onto the fact that they're now in the acting tuition business. But this is the way things work when you have a training contract with MI6, you sort of know you are working to save the country, but actually haven't been told so. The same goes for the characters in the series who make an impact on the readers. When you're writing the stuff, there's very little chance that you can pick them out from the start. Dave Wilcox is an excellent example of this in reverse. Whilst he's a part of the very high profile RSM's he's never really come out of his shell, apart from a few minor bit parts. But that's as they say... "is Showbiz." And Sammy, interesting to note that you've spent several years at drama school... it really does show in these rankings... I hope you get some "real" work soon!

19. Marko Ourigues;

He's a patronising bastard, as Alice would say, but you can't deny that Marko knows where he's from. If you polled fans on which character they would most like to sleep with in real life, the well-hung and eminently professional Boston/Brazilian would surely top the charts. Armed with a wolf fur rug, a patella hammer, and an endless supply of Caipirinhas, he's a dream come to life. (And Jamie's lisping portrayal just adds to the overall effect.) Last time we saw him, Marko invited Belinda to visit him in Rio, which disappointingly has not yet happened. Will we get to see inside his Amazon-based penis enlargement clinic? And will we be given any reason to believe it deserves its accreditation? Only time will tell.

Rocky's Comment;
I'm always in two minds whether to spell Marko with a "k" or with a "c" Marco, but the spelling of Ouriques is correct. This surname is based on some friends who live behind us in our seaside house in Northern Brazil. When they're all at the beach the gathered families number about 30 people, and boy do they know how to have fun. Classic Brazilians, the older folk are perhaps a little bit too religious for my taste, but, hey, why kick a culture. Marco himself is also based on a very good Brazilian friend, who did indeed get educated on a soccer scholarship in Boston. It's a real pity the similarity ends there as I'm sure he'd be making a lot more money as a top flight surgeon than he is today. But again, life can be like that, one day you're relaxing with a cold Skol beer on a hot windy beach and the next you're in lockdown in a cold and rainy London. Keep up the good work Marcko... I know Belinda will be visiting you and your home country very soon!

18. Maeve, aka Gunda, aka Trixie Forward, aka Agent XYZ;

The Irish honeybee seemed deceptively bland until she came of age with the introduction of "the hump and skunk". Unfortunately for Maeve, the plot required her to remain an enigma for several books, which didn't help her climb the rankings. However, a cavalcade of spectacular costume changes in the final reels propelled her up the charts. The sly nurse Gunda was a clever misdirection from Mr. Flintstone... although I'm amazed that Maeve was able to get approval to take leave from Steele's even as their International Sales Director had been kidnapped and the rest of the staff were hiding in a safe house. (Who would man the phones?) Then came Trixie Forward, who lived up to her name, although we have to assume she was wearing old lady prosthetics all the way down, if you know what I mean, to keep Belinda from guessing. As for her forest-floor catsuit, I'm still not sure what its purpose was, but after so much time in Lockdown, isn't it just nice to take these things out of the wardrobe once in a while? Maeve clearly started out with good intentions, but quickly turned bitter and jaded after she was denied an invite to Giselle's hen's do. We could get into a debate about whether an invite is mandatory for a new colleague you only met that same week, but it's clear that, in Maeve's mind, she was a monster created by the nepotistic nature of Steele's... and by the decision to invite Hazel. It's a moral lesson for us all. Could Maeve become Belinda's Hannibal Lecter, locked up and resentful, but forced to help her old nemesis when the going gets tough?

Rocky's Comment;
Some interesting comments here Sammy and I won't get too heavily into them because I want to keep the Irish mists of mystery swirling around Maeve for a little while longer. But what I do want to do is relate where In Ireland she came from in a sort of biological fashion, which goes some way to opening up a part of my timeline, albeit from the past, to you all. Here goes;

Agent 006.9X quietly swam away from the silent submarine at 024 hundred hours. It was a bitterly cold January night in 1944 and for all his exceptional spy skills he didn't succeed in his kilometre swim to land. His objective was a beach on the edge of the South Wicklow Hills of Ireland, but the stronger than normal currents denied him any chance of making it. However, the luck of the Irish came to his aid as an early morning salmon poacher found him entangled, unconscious, in his illegal fishing nets.

Bernard Brogan swore violently as he pulled the frozen German officer onboard his little boat, resenting the fact that another good nights' fishing had been ruined by the "Jerrys".

'God', he thought, 'if it's not the fuel pollution from their fuckin submarines, it's the bloody spies they send to land who keep fuckin up me nets.'

Bernard Blinked;

Agent 006.9X aged 24 and the youngest Colonel in the military was a tough nut, there were few tougher in the Wehrmacht but on that cold January morning he nearly didn't make it.

'God Berni... he's still freezing.' Bernard's wife Ursula cried.
Bernard stoically replied,
'Stick some more Bushmills whiskey into him... Jesus, sure we can barely afford to drink it ourselves, never mind dish it out to these bastards.'
He put some more wood on the already roaring fire, trying to get the room temperature above freezing.
'Kathleen!' he shouted, 'bring in more wood and some of that goat's milk you've been heating up!'
Kathleen, Bernard's and Ursula's only daughter, ran into the room doing her father's wishes. She sat down at the dying man's bedside and patiently spooned the hot liquid into his belly.

One year later;
'Kathleen!!' Ursula shouted, 'hurry yourself up... the wedding car's here.'
'I'm coming Ma... you can't leave without the bride you know!'
'Taach... Kathleen... sure you'd be late for your own funeral... never mind your wedding!' replied her mother proudly.
It was a grand affair for the sea faring Wicklow Hills folk... many said it was a marriage made in heaven.
Few knew the real truth.

You see, Kathleen's mad mixture of Goats Milk and Bushmills Whiskey had saved the young East Berlin spy's life… not that no one ever knew he was of that profession. Bernhardt as he was called, quickly realising he was onto a good thing with Kathleen, never mind the fairly decent cover the family had given him in the final months of the war with the Brits, had taken a fancy to his nurse. You see, Kathleen had tits like the teats of the Goat whose milk she'd plied him with at his worst hour. Her breasts were infinitely better, very much bigger and after a short recuperation period he discovered her resplendent flaming red vaginal glory in the family hayshed.

It had been decided from before their wedding day, much hastened by the impending birth of their first son, Kevin, that Bernhardt would become Bernard Brogan… a coincidence some would say with his father in laws own name… but as they say in Ireland…
'Sure, it is what it is…' accompanied with a knowing nod of the head, even though they didn't have a clue what they were talking about.
Bernhardt's impeccable English and ability to parrot any accent in the world, immediately made him a Wicklow Hills man and a little time after the end of the war he was able to initiate contact with his own dear family…
yes family…

Back in East Berlin now under Russian control, communications through the Irish Post Office were fraught and it was only many years later that his first letter made contact. His older brother Wolfgang had made a bit of an impact with his acquiring, at a very low cost, a well-established pots and pans manufacturing company in East Berlin and turning it, with the help of a little American investment, into a powerhouse of industrial pots and pans manufacturing. It seemed the world was his oyster, and it was. Within five years the company had grown massively and gained markets throughout the world. Wolfgang Bisch had become a rich and powerful man.

It was with some trepidation that Wolfgang picked up the tattered personal letter from his in tray some fifteen years after it had been posted. He immediately recognised the handwriting as that of his missing

in action brother. Tears ran down his bulbous cheeks as he read the short message from his long lost younger brother, Bernhardt.
'Dear Wolfgang, I hope this finds you well... now the war has been lost I shall visit you with my new wife Kathleen.'
Dein liebender bruder, Bernhardt.

Bisch screamed in delight and lit a cigar in celebration. From that day he determined to trace down his brother and meet this Kathleen who no doubt lived somewhere in Ireland.
'Yes family;'
He thought fondly.
Bisch Blinked;

It was a wet and windy July morning when Bernard Brogan met his brother Wolfgang off Lufthansa flight 6-69 at Dublin airport. This was the latest in a series of family get togethers over the years and the Bisch brothers never missed a chance to talk about the old days when they were growing up in East Berlin. But this was a very special day indeed; they were all attending the Christening of Bernard's second son Bill's newly arrived daughter. The brothers reminisced another proud family day when Bernard and Kathleen married Bill to Molly O'Hagan from Wicklow town itself.

Molly was the eldest daughter of a local supermarket owner who was buying other local shops and lately Bill had become key in advancing that expansion. Wolfgang was especially very proud of Bill and had been known to advance many Irish Punts in non-repayable loans to advance the fledgling business. However, this current occasion was all the sweeter, because Wolfgang was going to be Bill and Molly's daughter's Godfather. A role which tied the family together more than any other earthly bond could do.

At the short ceremony in the local church a proud Wolfgang held the little enfant in his arms.
'Dearly beloved,' the Priest intoned,
'we are gathered here to celebrate the christening of Maeve Brogan.'

Maeve Blinked;

Maeve Brogan Genealogy;

Grandfather;
Bernhardt Bisch latterly known as Brogan born 1920
Married Kathleen Brogan 1945

Father;
Bill (William) Brogan born 1950
Married Molly Brown 1980
Daughter Maeve Brogan born 1990

Godfather;
Wolfgang Bisch born in 1918

17. <u>Butch the Sunburnt Kid;</u>

Star of the most sensitively written cherry-plucking scene since de Sade, Butch (not his real name) got more than he bargained for on that motor yacht in sunny Spain. I was initially struck by Butch's dynamite good looks (James certainly lusts after him). My attention was further galvanised by his willingness to make witty comments about the four English tourists within their earshot. I liked him even more when I realised his ambitious nature... four women for your first time in the sack? That really is a fivesome's dream! And I was sent over the edge by his boldness, asking for work experience at the height of his first carnal encounter. I wonder where my life would be right now if I'd followed the example set by this suave Swede.

Rocky's Comment;
Yes, Butch is a young man on the way up. Similar to Sam the Youngish Manager he doesn't take no for an answer. Good looking, primed and honed into a taught sexual machine by Belinda Blumenthal, he has his whole life before him. Guaranteed success due to his ability to speak three languages... well perhaps his Spanish needed a bit of practice, but his Swedish and English are beyond question... he even understands the sex words. I recently had an email from Abbie asking about his progress or lack of progress in the books. This is what she wrote...

"I just had a thought I wanted to share with you Rocky.
In S3E12 Belinda has a wonderful time with the suave Butch the Sunburnt Kid, and at the end of their dalliance the conversation goes;
Butch: "What do you do for a job Belinda?"
Belinda "I'm an international sales director for a pots and pans company"
Butch: "International? That's interesting. Can I have some work experience?"
... and the chapter simply ends there, never to be spoken of again.
I was wondering, now that it seems like Belinda is the owner of Bisch Herstellung, could Butch the Sunburnt Kid finally get his opportunity to have some work experience with Belinda? He'd make a great new addition to the new team as a fresh young intern, and he was clearly intrigued by the international aspect of the job! We'd have a Swede in Germany speaking English! And perhaps now he's matured enough to be eligible for

*a spot of work experience… and Belinda could then be the one
interviewing him like in Chapter 1 Book 1!
Rocky, as you know, we all have our favourite one-hit-wonders from the
novels such as Alfie the smallish man, Zachariah, Hans & Greta etc… and
as always, we expect cameos in new books but I feel this one would make
so much sense! Though, I don't know how Rocky? that is… Rocky!"*

I love getting these sort of emails… so refreshing from the day to day
grind. Thanks Abbie!

BUT… Sammy and Abbie… you haven't heard the news? I'm truly sorry to
be the one who's breaking this to you, but Butch is dead… he's done his
last Sundance. Here's what we know happened, though the source… Bill in
HR is always a bit dubious. A few weeks after Butch's encounter with the
Glee Team he was lost at sea in a violent storm such as the Mediterranean
can quickly throw up. To be honest, it took a while for the news to get
back to the Steeles offices. Bill in HR found out first as he had Butch's CV
and had invited him for an interview. On not getting a reply he contacted
his parents and was told the terrible news… The only small sliver of hope
is that his body was never recovered… perhaps he's somewhere on a
desert island in N. Africa? We can but hope! Is this a new mission for the
reunited Glee Team?

16. Clint;

Belinda's high school paramour was the best new character to appear in book six. Every line is eminently quotable and his dopey stoner voice is a thing of beauty. It's unclear why Clint seems to be stuck in the late 1970s, but the night of passion between the foxy mama and the Wibbly Wobbly Wonder left me no room for complaint. The more I think about Clint (and I do), I can't help wondering what happens when he runs out of room for new tattoos. He apparently adds one to his collection every time he has nookie, but he's already reached the point where post-coital lovers have to ink his scrotum. Will he have to stop with the nookie? Dare he ink over the existing ones? Does he have to start piercing himself instead? Good luck out there, you beautiful moron.

Rocky's Comment;
Clint is one of those characters who come quickly... pardon the coarse pun... and go as quickly in the story. However, he has actually achieved immortality as Mouldy Wood, the artist responsible for all the book covers, has encapsulated him forever in the Belinda Blinked Book 6 front cover. (You can purchase a personally signed poster by me on my Etsy Store called "RockysPavilion".)
https://www.etsy.com/uk/listing/1067443451/
Even Toffee Apple Chew and Jail Man haven't yet had this accolade. Thank you Mouldy for another stunning interpretation of the books. Clint is a no hoper, but that's what we see today, perhaps back in time when he and Belinda got it together, he was a high-flying ambitious student who got caught up in the torrid grip of drugs. It does happen all too frequently as I'm sure we all have had personal experiences of. So, let's hope with his new found fame he can get some therapy, clean up his act and earn enough money for Marco Ouriques to do his thing in his Amazonian theatre of miracles. One thing's for sure, Belinda will not be paying for it!

15. Alfie Small;

Who is Alfie Small, aka the Smallish Man Dressed in Black, sound man to the stars? His wiring technique is nonconformist, true, but I haven't seen any better options on *The Generation Game* lately. And isn't it dull to just stick the lapel mic on the lapel? Boring! If you want to know more, find Alfie on Linkedin. It'll be super duper.

Rocky's Comment;
Alfie Small used to use pins for attaching his mics to his victims, and then one day he burst a bubble… well he actually stuck one into a human body. The shrieking and wailing was so intense he's been a sticky tape man ever since. Lucky Belinda encountered him after his conversion, otherwise it could have been a very bloody presentation to Claus Bloch's ladies. I find it amazing that Alphie… was that a slip of the pen??? has gained the notoriety he has, just by saying he can be contacted via Linkelin, whatever that is. I personally would have left my cell number, but hey ho?

14. Mistress Sweetjuice;

This Parisian mademoiselle is the roly-poly, food-obsessed, Flump-tailed star attraction at the Moulin Marron. Oh, you haven't heard of it? Bloody tourist! Rocky is a champion for body positivity, reminding us that all ages, shapes, and sizes can be sexy, and when that bundle of balloons descended from the ceiling, Mistress Sweetjuice proved to be his strongest statement on the subject. (Spare a thought for the cleaners, though. Bite-sized pieces of ham, cheese, and baguette are a nightmare to get rid of.) Sweetjuice has chosen not to follow society's norms, and I'm here for it. She's also chosen not to follow modern science's pesky recommendations about refrigerating dairy products, and I leave that decision up to the individual reader.

Rocky's Comment;
Mistress... perhaps now "Madame" as she's made the big time by appearing (one night only) in the series. Note I don't count a rogue appearance as a talent spotter in a pretty low budget English pantomime as a proper assignment. No Mistress Sweetjuice is, as her description, a lovely person who has made acting with wires her signature talent. The pieces of ham, cheese and French bread falling all around, were actually a mistake as they were her lunch. Unfortunately, the degradable plastic bag she carried them in, decided to biodegrade at the wrong time. But as we all can appreciate that is how genius appears. It's now of course the crescendo to her new act which is proving very popular with the Parisienne public. It seems to me Marie Antoinette should have forgotten the "let them eat cake" line and gone with Sweetjuices interpretation of "let them eat cheese, ham and bread..." now there's a thought!

13. Sir James Godwin;

After his wife died in a tragic(?) parachute(??) accident(???), Sir James could have given up his ambitions and given in to his grief. Instead, he committed his life to raising funds for the asses and donkeys of the world while building Steele's into the second largest distributor of pots and pans in Europe. (Next stop: overtaking Hido Sakie.) With a voice that puts him somewhere between Boris Johnson and Prince Philip (may he rest in peace), and the power to bring down governments if traffic on the roads gets too much, Sir James has always been somewhat cantankerous. But he seemed to be on Team Belinda until his astonishing behaviour in the season six finale. I'm highly tempted to toss him further down these rankings. But he's been cagey before... compare with the time when he feigned a heart attack to get Belinda to Australia... so I highly suspect that this is all a wheeze (as Rocky would say) and the truth about his attitude and his wife's death will be worth the wait.

Rocky's Comment;
Sir James is an interesting character in the series... and not just because he's at #13. As the senior in the boardroom he really shouldn't be carrying as much plot as he does. But he's totally fascinating and there's so much back plot to catch up with. If we start at the beginning... well here it is...

Sir James Godwin; February 1963

The weather was cold... no not cold... freezing. The youngish James Godwin looked at his specially manufactured sub-zero fluorescent watch.... there was thankfully only 30 minutes to go. He put down his sniper's rifle and blew on his hands. He knew he had to keep them supple, his objective demanded it. He picked up the rifle and looked through the state of the art, telescopic sights where everything was magnified 200 times. He calmly scanned the footpath 153 feet below him pausing only at the sexily flightish woman selling candles. She'd been there for two hours now... but more importantly; she'd sold nothing, nada, nix... even with her stunning looks. She was either going to starve... or she was undercover. Yes, undercover...

Now whilst James Godwin had been an operative for only three months, he was no dumbo, he'd done his homework and he knew that the best operatives the Soviets had, always hid in plain sight. A sexually attractive woman selling candles was a superb cover... even for the Commies.

Wolfgang Bisch was glad he'd wrapped up real tight as this was his first operation where he had control of a couple of operatives. Two females... both like himself; Berliners... East Berliners come to that... one largish and one flighty. He didn't care, he was in control. Over the past couple of months in training school he'd learnt that purpose was all about control. Indeed, if you really thought about it, control was purpose... he shook the brainwashing thoughts out of his head. He was here to neutralise and the foreign agent he was after was very close, but where...

On the street the flighty Birgit groaned, she'd now been fully in place for well over two hours. What the fuck was Bisch doing... or not doing... he was an imbecile, everyone in training school knew this. Why was he leading the operation, it just didn't make sense. Birgit felt frustrated, she hadn't sold a candle; fuck it, she hadn't even made eye contact with anyone who wanted to buy a candle. That meant it had to be a shoot out and from her training she was the most exposed... she knew at that moment that if she stayed here, she was going to die... Besides it was too cold and no sensible candle seller would be out on the street. She'd become suspicious to even any casual onlooker, never mind a trained foreign agent... and her training told her so.

Up on the ledge James Godwin felt the first flecks of snow tickle his neck, 'Fuck it,' he thought, 'even the elements are against me.'
But Godwin was not one to deviate from instructions and the man he was sent to cancel out had not yet shown his face. But James's window of escape only remained open for another twenty-three minutes. The Town Hall clock was ticking and he started to slightly sweat even in the intense cold.

The street scene changed, a dazzling slightly older woman walked past the candle seller, turned and re-paced her steps.
'Do you sell candles?'
The candle seller gasped, and said,
'Ya... I have a large collection.'
'But you are so beautiful, why are you doing this job?'

The candle seller agent blushed, the older woman exuded a sense of awe, she was obviously experienced in all the laws of sex, but why was she saying this… was she another agent… a double bluff from Bisch, or a second British Agent perhaps?

'It's what my family do…. we sell candles…' she blustered, sticking to her spy story training under the aura of this mysterious woman.

'I see…. would you like to sell your body in Amsterdamm…. with me, now, no going back… what do you think? You can call me Zara.

The candle seller stood up stiffly and pocketed her revolver, she'd had enough, Bisch could go to hell, she was going to Amsterdamm to sell her body and possibly a few candles in the right place for real money… and the opportunity to suck the hell out of this stranger's tits.

Birgit Blinked;

James Godwin noted the exit of the candle seller with the flirtatious older woman, this was unusual he thought. He'd better be extra careful; the Commies were obviously up to something so devious even training school hadn't seen what was coming next. He tightened his grip on his rifle and concentrated even harder. Even so he thought briefly about Special Agent Maia and how he'd screwed her so hard into the bed that morning and then how she'd satisfied him so deeply that he was late in leaving the safe house. He shook his head and his squinting eye swept the grey concrete buildings opposite looking for his quarry.

Wolfgang Bisch was now openly fuming,

'What the fuck was Agent Birgit doing leaving her post in the middle of a critical operation with this flashy woman. It was suicide… for him, he'd planned for her to take the bullets and now she'd just pissed off. Bisch swore profusely and lit a cigarette; Godwin saw the match flare 200 metres away and instantly took the shot. Bisch cried out in pain as the bullet ricocheted against the concrete wall and ended up in his upper arm. He'd been wounded, and even worse it hadn't even been a clean shot, shards of concrete were the worst. He shouted out in agony and passed out.

James Godwin broke down the rifle into its constituent pieces and stuffed them into concealed pockets under his clothing. He'd astutely decided earlier that morning to do without the carrying case… it would be too obvious. That decision saved his life. He exited the building and pulled his soviet style cap down over his eyes. He instantly froze, a largish East German woman with gimlet eyes wearing heavy black shoes glanced at him as she shuffled past the front door of the apartment block. The snow was starting to lie, and her dragging footprints stood out as warning signs to any competent spy; James Godwin had now passed into that category. His mission accomplished, all he had to do was execute his exit plan.

'Oh James, you are such a tease...'
Back in London, James Godwin turned over in the bed and looked at his latest girlfriend, Julia, full in the eye,
'You're calling me a tease Julia... are you sure you want to continue in this vein?'
'Yes... you are a tease.... you never tell me about your work, you disappear off without a moment's notice and you come back all beaten up... I just can't believe you... if I didn't know you were a professional sports person I'd say you were a spy.'
James laughed and grabbed Julia's tits,
'Come on trouble maker; let's give you a right proper lesson in spy-craft.'
James rolled over on top of her and put his hand onto her vagina. She squealed ever so gently and acquiesced to his advances. Her clit moistened and he put his lips to her labia, his tongue moved slowly up and down continuing to tease her. Julia lay back, relaxed and opened her legs further; she was going to enjoy this...

James Blinked;

Wolfgang Bisch lay in his hospital bed. The Surgeon Colonel had just finished his visit and the news was not good, his upper arm would never fully heal. Mould growing on the concrete wall where the lone bullet had initially hit, together with the concrete fragments, had started a chain reaction with his red blood cells; the rest was down to nature and the surgeon's skill. Bisch's mind worked overtime, the western agent had to die and he wouldn't rest until he'd tracked him down and shot him like a dog in the gutter.

Bisch Blinked;

<u>12. Lieutenant George Sylvester, aka Georgie Porgie; aka Giles Cottonsberth;</u>

To quote James Cooper:
"Why is George Sylvester the most fleshed-out character in the Belinda Blinked books?"
Can we blame George for his traumatic backstory? After his mother succumbed to yellow fever, George grew up in the care of his stiff-upper-lip father, a military veteran, who only wanted a similar life for his two sons. His brother Tony was in the secretive SAS for a few years but was always more interested in business than family, and was never around for him during those traumatic teenage years. So, George joined the military, just to make all the pain go away. Instead, in his later career, he was kidnapped in Africa whilst working for a mercenary outfit codenamed Greensword International and held for ransom. A ransom which, astoundingly, Colonel Sylvester refused to pay... or didn't have the resources to pay, leaving his son presumed dead. In his weakened physical and psychological state he suffered Stockholm syndrome and Lieutenant George was recruited by the terrorists. Between that and being cursed with a tight frenulum of prepuce of penis, one could argue that the mongrel from Manchester never had a choice. George gave us some of the series' most self-aware lines and he helped string out the Bisch arc over three books because of his gross incompetence. Sadly, that same frenulum is no more, brutally snapped off at gunpoint, causing what can only have been an agonising death. I can't believe I just wrote that sentence.

Rocky's Comment;
Hey Sammy... at #12 in the rankings I thought you would be getting used to those sort of sentences... this, after all, is Belinda Blinked. Do you now feel like Jamie does? Every day is a new learning curve... ha ha ha...
Yes, Georgie Porgie, as encapsulated in song by many songsmiths when the capture of Professor Slinz was podcasted, is another deep dive of a character. "Pack your bags and Slinz..."
I wanted to bring in our family background of having lived in Manchester UK for, let's say, nearly 35 years. Not that any of us were involved in the military, or... God forbid, the business of criminality.
Is being a Regional Sales Manager criminal?

Some would say yes... others, no... perhaps going to the Club Theatre every Saturday morning and learning acting is...

Georgie is the brother from hell... he's obviously always been difficult, but when your family gets a $2 million ransom note... well what would you do? The fact that they buried the situation and walked away perhaps says more about Georgie than anything else. He was trouble from the word go. By the time we get the tap tapping on the stone flags at the back of the church where his brother is getting married and a couple of sentences before that, Belinda communing with God and him nodding in reply, well we're onto a helter-skelter of future time lines. Add the Jim Stirling incident with the wedding cake and you can see that the story was really getting out of control. Literally a writer's nightmare!

Georgie Porgie was then revealed to have stolen his brother's new bride and between them, the Tri Oxy Brillo range pots and pans blueprints. How much deeper could he have plunged the knife of revenge into Tony's heart I dare not say. In a final series of twists the story switched internationally... namely Australia where he committed his deepest sin... the death of James Sp00ner, beloved for some time by Belinda. From there Georgie Porgie the character goes rapidly downhill... reduced to a nonentity called Giles Cottonsberth it was obvious his end was nigh. How fitting it was that the Glee Team were there to see his final destruction at the hands of another unknown Bisch protegee.
Now Sammy, whilst that last sentence was difficult, it was so, so, necessary and apt.
Business is brutal Mr Yeo!!

11. James "Sp00ns" Sp00ner, aka Mr. James Tea, the Much Honoured, Laird of Gretna Green;

We discovered as early as the book four finale that Sp00ner was just a bit... shit. In spite of sounding like Sean Connery and possessing an enviable array of gadgets (fold-out wet wipes, anyone?), Sp00ner...
failed to identify the Special One;
failed to catch the Special One;
failed to protect Slinz;
failed to save the Blueprints;
failed to notice the two traitors folding a body into the trunk of their car right in front of him;
failed to capture the sickly Bisch at the Schloss;
failed to rescue Belinda and Bella from Jailman;
failed to clarify to his many ex-wives the order in which he had last slept with them.
Do I need to go on?

Aside from successfully tutoring Agent "Smiffy" Blumenthal in the ways of spy-craft, I'm not sure Sp00ner was worth his fee. (Perhaps if I wanted an apartment made from croissants, but that's a different skill entirely.) But also... RIP, Sp00ns. He's strumming his E-class lyre in heaven now. Once a year, I'll get out my spoons and play Mozart's Requiem at the end of my driveway for you. Hope he didn't forget Peggy Loveleaf in his will.

Rocky's Comment;
Whilst it's in my mind, I'm really glad Peggy Loveleaf didn't make the ratings... my Chardonnay befuddled mind has to ask, did she even make the books?
Never mind, the real subject is James Sp00ner... did anyone ever get the double zero in the way his name was spelt? Probably not, but it proves he was born to be a 00.
Personally, I really enjoyed the part Sp00ner played in the books, as Sammy noted, he started out so well as an IT professional and ... well, it just went downhill all the way. Perhaps it was just a wrong career choice, he should have joined a photocopier maintenance company and developed a skill for rescuing beleaguered Key Account Managers from carbonizing themselves.

But MI6 called and Sp00ns was not found to be lacking. His very name totally suited the assignment, spoons, pots and pans… perhaps I should introduce a villain named Fork… or Knife? Whatever, it was a very sad time for me when I realised that he was no more fit for purpose… his death was inevitable. Sammy, you've called it… he failed at virtually every opportunity, why he could have saved 3 books worth of dialogue if he'd caught out Giselle at that water pumping works in North London… did someone shout… Cricklewood?

In the literary world it's always hard to kill off one of the major characters in a book. Mainly because you cannot bring them back again. I know that many authors do by going back in time or some such other technique, but I feel that that's cheating the reader or listener. I've always thought that the Xmas Special where he assists Belinda in assessing the true impact of her life on earth on the people around her was as close as I'd get to his revival. But to be honest perhaps his character suits that of being a ghost, surrounded by swirling mist as he helps Belinda manoeuvre her way through her torrid task of being head of Bisch Herstellung. There's one big flaw in all of this though and it's one of Alice's favourite comments, "where is the sex?"

Yes, it's pretty difficult for a ghost to have sex with someone still on this earth… but I suppose I should try and push the sexual taboo boundaries just a bit further. To be honest, I do have a sneaking deep felt admiration for Sp00ns and his tootling around heaven on his 50cc lyre, he could so easily have let Belinda have her way and die, that way they'd both be ghosts and no doubt sexually compatible. Perhaps God has strict rules about post death sexual activity… no doubt we'll all find out in our own time. But for now, I'm still plotting Sp00ner's after life and how he can still play his part in Belinda's future… or not. As I'm currently writing Book 10, I can't give too much away though my current timelines extend past Book 11…

But Sammy… I didn't know you played the Sp00ns… with me on the harmonica and your talent we could lay down a couple of tracks no problem…. "Will ye go lassie go?"

10. Jail Man;

A man of simple pleasures, an eye for the Sheilas, and a penchant for long narratives. Am I talking about Rocky Flintstone or Jail Man? Agatha Christie created her own doppelgänger in the character of Ariadne Oliver. Cervantes and Martin Amis wrote themselves into their works. And Jail Man seems like another in that long-line of authors inspired by themselves. I know Rocky claims to most identify with Sir James Godwin, the alleged puppet-master, but this Australian raconteur feels like a closer match to me. Next time I'm stuck on an endless road trip (or hot air balloon ride), all I'll need is a hot cup of spiced water noodles and some Jail Man stories, and I'm set. (Perhaps the less said the better about his relationship with the Big Book of Clink Procedures™.)

Rocky's Comment;
The top ten... well, this is where the big characters hang out, and for a character who only spoke a handful of words, Jail Man is really hitting above his weight. A contractor to Herr Bisch I do hope he got paid for his sordid duties in keeping two English beauties locked up in his clink. Of course, he surpassed his initial job description of just keeping jail, by interning the internationally famous spy, James Sp00ner, in a bit of quick jail door ballet. It proved to be Sp00ners last mistake as shortly after he was dead from George's knife attack. Pity Jail Man couldn't have played fair and kept his prisoner alive just a little bit longer. But it wasn't to be and if I truly am Jail Man in the books, I wouldn't want to be the slob he so obviously is. Give me a smartly dressed Des Martin or Patrick O'Hamlin any day of the week please Sammy. Of course, if Jail Man wants a bit of assistance in self-publishing his massive repertoire of smutty stories, then it would be churlish of me not to assist. So on a positive note, let's wait and see what Jail Man's got up his sleeve... jus clinkin...

<u>9. Giselle Maarschalkerweerd de Klotz, aka the Special One;</u>

Prior to season six, Giselle would not have made my Top 10. She was a traitor to the cause, committing flagrant betrayal and grim atrocities all in the name of raising funds for experimental research into one of the less publicised (and less pronounceable) dermatological conditions. Realising the seriousness of the situation for her former Glee Team pals, The Bald One chose to redeem herself, although indications are that Steele's is still feeling pretty cautious about her. I say they should be more sympathetic.

As we've seen with her fellow turncoats, Maeve and George, there's usually a tragic backstory, and I think Giselle is no different. Remember that we didn't know about her genital disease until the McDonagh brothers came along. No-one did: not Tony, not Belinda. Doesn't this suggest that she was deeply sexually unsatisfied? Living a humdrum existence, lying awake in her bedsit each night longing for the kind of unfettered, kinky, exhibitionist behaviour that her traditional Belgian-slash-Dutch family had suppressed in her. Giselle had dreams, and they were left empty and unfulfilled.
When we consider it from this angle, was it all that wrong for her to betray;
her best friends;
her husband;
her employer;
and her country?
To cause multiple deaths?
To maintain an ongoing pen-pal relationship with a psychopath?

If you've never thought about doing any of the above, I'd be surprised. Having said that, Giselle's rehabilitation isn't confirmed just yet, so this is a tentative position on the leader board. But with a little faith, and confidence born of her new Vidal Bassoon wig, Giselle could still make it from PA to Managing Director in 5 years. One can only hope.

Rocky's Comment;
Hope... yes, that's what keeps us all going, and Giselle needs tons and tons of it. The problem is she's been sidelined in the Steeles Pots and Pans hierarchy. I do not see Tony promoting her to Managing Director anytime

soon... if ever. No, all Giselle has left is hope. I am however pleased that she's back in the Glee Team, Belinda and Bella enjoy themselves much more raucously when Giselle is around. OK... she's always got a sarcastic comment to make about one or other of the other two, but deep down she's still a friend... or is she? Giselle is always going to look out for herself and if things don't happen her way, then she'll use all her skillset to change the situation. That's just the way she is and nothings gonna change that any time soon.

As you all know, the Glee Team are the glue in the Steeles organisation, always pissed after 4pm, up for a good time, and ready to strip off for any opportunity where pots and pans sales can be increased. Truly loyal employees, but just when we get them back together again, another one leaves, this time it's Belinda. Of course, I'm sure they'll remain friends, but new company rivalries will make it more difficult. Perhaps they'll meet up when Belinda flies into the UK on business, after all the Pentra is ideally situated for this to happen pretty regularly.

Speaking of which Sammy, why is the Pentra not in these rankings... surely it's got more character than let's say... Jail Man? At the very worst, it's had more words written about the place than Jail Man has ever had. It's just a question... Sammy can I live in hope?

So, Giselle Maarschalkerweerd de Klotz is still an unknown entity and her story has a long way to go, unlike Bella? who has probably peaked... see below. Giselle's surname is also the longest of all the characters and that was deliberate, it made calling her the Special One an utter delight as I still to this day cannot spell her full name without referring to the first time, I wrote it down... the same was true for Herstellung, but thankfully I've now mastered that one.

Giselle for me is a tortured soul crying out for deliverance from all the wrongs of her life to date...

joining the Glee Team;
marrying Tony;
meeting George;
suffocating Slinz;
working for Bisch;
stealing Bisch's money;
travelling to Australia;
wearing a wig;
re-joining Steeles Pots and Pans;

But... it all makes for an intoxicating future and we need to ask, what else can she cock up in her life? For those of you who are about to ask the obvious question, no, she is not a member of COCK and never will be??

8. Agent Helga Jonker;

Helga was compelling from her debut appearance, emerging from her cupboard to whip up her famous mayonnaise. And she went full method during her first encounter with Belinda, convincingly portraying a frumpy sexual novice with incredibly efficient skills at contract document binding. Since then, she has offered surprise after surprise, revealing herself to be an FBI angel with a penchant for astonishing undercover work: frail crone, background welder, the woman can do it all. She's had some less brilliant moments, too. Her willingness to let a stranger up to her hotel room while hiding out from a bad spy guy wasn't great. And if there was ever a time to go without a bit of slap-and-tickle, it's when you're revealing time-sensitive insider information in the toilets during a wedding. But as we know, moles who've been undercover for a long time start to make sloppy mistakes. Can't blame her. Given that Bisch and co have been put to rights, this may be the last we see of this sassy Yankee Southerner... or whatever she was, the voice wasn't all that consistent. But it was a good time while it lasted.

Rocky's Comment;
Deep cover in plain sight is the best way any surveillance should be... ask anyone in the espionage business. That's why I so enjoyed the later discovered fact that not only was Helga playing this game, but her boss Dr Robbins was as well. Little has been made of this amazing coincidence and I just wanted to put it out there.
However, I suspect the FBI chiefs might now be reassessing Helga's unique abilities in the field and surely a recall back to Langley is well overdue. Indeed, seeing she has good contacts with Belinda and her MI6 boss, the Duchess, promotion seems overdue. After all, both sides need to keep the old alliance alive and kicking. Let's take a look at those abilities in the following FBI report about her boss Dr Robbins... Wayne Burt...

United Sates Department of Justice
Federal Bureau of Investigation
Field Office Local Attaches; Amsterdam
Classification; Confidential;

Case file No. 76 AM 18
Activity classification ; 76 Escaped Federal Prisoner;
Subject; Doctor, Robbins, Pieter
Nationality; American;
Crime; Fraud against USA Army Units of the Rhine;
Zone of Operation; Europe;
Copy to; Director FBI Washington DC
        Date 07 07 1993
Agent; Helga Jonker

Synopsis;
Dr Pieter Robbins is Purchasing Director of Rouse Supermarkets
based in Amsterdam. He is my immediate boss in this organisation.
My role in this company is part of my deep cover in Europe and it is
through it I have uncovered this extraordinary crime. In his job as
purchasing Director Dr. Robbins receives many approaches for the
supply of goods. These pass through my office. The offer of
10,000,000 cans of tinned beans from the US Army of the Rhine was
my first piece of incriminating evidence. Dr Robbins signed the
purchase order and the goods were duly shipped to the Rouse
supermarket chain over a period of two years. I have been unable
to discover where the payments have arrived. Further investigation
of Dr Robbins has meanwhile unearthed an uncanny likeness to an
escaped Federal prisoner from the US Army of the Rhine. This
prisoner named Wayne Burt working in the Quartermaster section,
was waiting transportation back to the US on fraud charges when
he escaped just over twelve years ago. My investigations are still at
an early stage and are thus inconclusive.

Forward Action;
To continue investigating Dr Robbins/Wayne Burt. To send the
information to our Fraud section regarding the payments for the
tinned beans. Investigate the Wayne Burt fraud case and evidence
against him.

Washington DC action request;

Permission to advance scrutiny of unsub and his past misdemeanours in the US army. Send fraud section in New York payment information.

Copies to;
Washington; file case No.   76 HQ 5297
Bureau New York overseas station; file case No.   76 NY 276
Amsterdam Field office; file case no; 76 AM 18

An FBI agent in action... but we must also understand that whilst Rouse Supermarkets purchased ten million cans of beans, Wayne was also supplying his own fast food shops known as Burts Baked Beans, throughout East Germany. To be honest... that could well be another 30 million cans... some scam... Come on Helga, full marks, at least you got there with Belinda's help in the end.

7. Jim Stirling;

As far as American moguls with small appendages, dubious approaches to business, and frail masculinity go, Stirling is one of the better ones. Who would've thought, on his first rather inauspicious appearance, that the Vole Master would become a candidate for Belinda's most compatible sexual partner? (She doesn't do boyfriends, or I'd say "love of her life".) This Yankee is unquestionably loyal and rampantly horny, although it's concerning that he'd have no qualms about requesting keys to his guests' hotel rooms in the middle of the night. He likes 'em bare, and he must really be racking up the frequent flyer points, as Jim seems to visit England at the drop of a cowboy hat, somehow arriving in time for the COCK meeting which was scheduled with only 6.3 hours' notice! Size doesn't matter, and the podcasters have made clear in later episodes that it was the vole's presentation rather than its dimensions that sent them gagging. But for the sake of Jim's confidence, it's comforting to know that he's now a big boy. His neon blue ejaculation was responsible for perhaps the single most poetic sentence ever written by that literary legend Rocky Flintstone:
"Jim was rubbing her just right, and Belinda gave into nature... not once, but twice... before the inevitable blue ejaculation cut across her dreams."

Rocky's Comment;
Jim Stirling is a sterling sort of guy and the character for whom I've taken the most criticism. And rightly so... as I mentioned in my co lab book with the podcast crew called, funnily enough, "My Dad Wrote a Porno" available signed by myself through my Etsy store... RockysPavilion
But yes, criticism regarding why I decided to make Jim with his small appendage American, and more than that, a citizen of the State of Texas... where, we are reliably informed on this side of the pond, everything is very large. No kidding... So, in line with my crazy concepts of all things Belinda Blinked, it was a no bummer decision to make Jim a Yank. However, I did initially toy all those years ago of making Jim French. It would have kept the maze scene nice and tight with all three gentlemen coming from Europe. But then I thought of my potential market place with regarding to future book sales and I realised very few "Frenchies" speak English never mind actually read a book. I also didn't want to cause a diplomatic incident by labelling a successful French industrialist as

someone with a small cock. The French can get very touchy about such things even though they have some of the most beautiful small women in the world... think Penelope Pollet! So, it was decided that I'd let the American Texan take the hit, and I'm glad I did, because he rose manfully to the job and has become a great character in the books.

Some of the best incidents in the books involve Jim and here I'm thinking about Belinda's concern regarding the flossing of her teeth after the flaky skin visit at his head office. The wedding cake slip up is another great conversation starter for all "Belinkers" and I believe the sales of blue icing for wedding cakes have gone through the roof... go figure. But, perhaps the best of those is where we meet him first, in the muddy maze, and whilst he doesn't speak, the mental image of Belinda straining to satisfy him as she wonders if he's actually inside her has hit the spot so to speak for so many fans...

6. Toffee Apple Chew;

This soul sister stallion romped into our hearts at the end of book four and has never looked back. TACy is a fierce fighter but also a solemn companion during periods of mourning. Her empathy is at the rather high end of the equine spectrum, able to sense the joyous or sorrowful mood of the moment with precision. Sadly, she wasn't able to join the gang in Australia due to that country's strict quarantine regulations, and that FOMO may have been what led to her subsequent cider addiction. (I'm not judging you, girl.) As for the implication at the state funeral that Toffee Apple Chew enjoyed Sp00ner riding her a little *too* much, I say a girl's gotta take it where she can get it.

Rocky's Comment;
For those of you who don't already know, TACy as she's happily known, is a horse... OK, you may have guessed this since Sammy referred to a soul sister stallion... technically wrong Sammy as a stallion in my farming world is a male and TACy is definitely female. This of course is why she's so good at having high levels of empathy... most females the world over, far outweigh the men in this trait. Whilst she doesn't drink "Chards" I'm pretty certain she's taken care of the Duchess on many occasions when she's had one too many for the road or the jumping arena. Who else would have taken care of the Duchess the afternoon Belinda left her sprawling naked on the gravel outside Epsom Hall? Toffee Apple Chew certainly had her ears pricked for the return of her Mistress and what a state she was in. Those massive nipples would have been dragging on the ground as the pissed Duchess inched her way up the front steps to her bedrooms. Imagine the scene if Duke Clarence had discovered her slithering her way across the central wood floored hall. It certainly wouldn't have been good for the staff, or her continued presence at MI6. No, instead the faithful TACy dragged her back to the stables, licked her clean of driveway dust and let her sleep it off on a warm bed of hay. A true companion in a time of dire need.

5. Herr Wolfgang Bisch

Is there a character in all of Dickens, Tolstoy, Zola, or Shakespeare who can rival the unfiltered, unmitigated, utterly disgusting evil of Wolfie B? He's propelled by one of Jamie's most evocative voices, possesses an insatiable desire to have his employees murder one another, and constantly emits a range of charming excretions. (A diet of Bavarian cheeses and hams and sour trout will do that to you.) Bisch has no redeeming qualities whatsoever. Well, *almost none*: his tastefully decorated schloss with its sex dungeon, slides between storeys, and frescoes on the ceiling, sounds like an ideal place to party. Book six opened the floodgates on this business Herr's backstory, revealing that he has been utterly dishonourable for decades. When he wasn't scheming to deprive our troops of their dietary fibre, he was hunting the globe for his step-niece with malevolent intent. (I would've started looking where her parents lived, but that's just me.) Herr Bisch is in chains now, and there doesn't seem much chance he'll be able to acquire the millions of Marks he would need to break himself free. Still, he casts a long shadow over the series. Really, Bisch is a triumph of the imagination. A very sick imagination, to be clear, but a triumph nevertheless.

Rocky's Comment;
Every good story needs a good baddie and Herr Bisch is a good one. The James Godwin reveal, a few pages ago, shows just how twisted Bisch really is. His brother Bernard Brogan isn't really far behind him and we have still yet to assess the actions of Maeve his young blood relative. Belinda also being a relative of Bisch has somehow managed to avoid the malevolent genes lurking in the family tree. One has to wonder how long that situation can last as she gets to grips with Bisch's life's work Bisch Herstellung. If only Bisch hadn't decided to blood the young Maeve so deeply into his mire that she too ended up in the clink. Maeve would have been a much more natural successor to the floundering behemoth as she is truly a direct descendent.
But of course, as we all now know Bisch's mind is too devious for straight thinking. His compulsive hatred of Sir James Godwin and his desire to steal the ground breaking technology from Steeles lead him down a path which ended in his very own destruction. But to be honest, it was touch and go, the recruitment of "The Special One" from inside the Steele inner

circle was genius and only a very last minute, change of heart by Giselle saved the day. Of course, his recruitment of George Sylvester was another deep swipe at the Steeles management tree. No one could ever have thought that Tony's long disappeared brother would have been found by Bisch and rescued from incarceration by a payment much reduced from the initial valuation of George's worth to his family. Yes, George was very close to Wolfgang Bisch, but he was too much the criminal to ever inherit the Bisch empire. In time Bisch saw through George's lying and made his biggest mistake… the placement of Maeve to replace Giselle. We know how it eventually played out with all Bisch's associates ending up in the clink, no doubt being looked after by Jail man… God help us, it might just take a handful of Ozzie dollars to engineer all their release and the baddies will be back in business. Who knows, but Bisch will surely be long gone, now in his mid-nineties, death is surely just lurking around the next corner.

<u>4. Des Martin, aka Santa Claus (Papa Noel, etc.);</u>

If Bisch is the most evil figure in literature, Des may be the most pathetic. Strangely, he *was* high-performing and seemingly debonair when Belinda arrived at the company. In the aftermath of her appearance on the scene, he totalled his car, lost his marriage, nearly quit his job, saw his manhood reduced to a frozen stub in a stationery cupboard, dedicated his weekends to wearing a full chauffeur outfit in order to ferry the boss around town, was violently injured in a car explosion (oh sorry, it was only a surface wound), *and* released untold gallons of bodily fluid across London and the South-East. And all of this because of his boss' juicy pomegranates. Notice how, as soon as Belinda was removed from her job (if you're going to go missing, presumed dead, you have to face the consequences), he began a meteoric rise to the top again? Few novelists would choose to have their main character be the cause of a nice guy's total wrack and ruin, which is a real marker of the level of commitment Rocky has to his work. It's why we all keep coming back, year after year. Year after gruelling year.

Rocky's Comment;
Gruelling is a good word to describe Des Martin's love life, well... perhaps non-existent is a better one. Perhaps that's why he's the highest placed male in these rankings... no mean feat Sexy Dez!! But he does seem to keep going against all the odds and it's stamina and true grit like this that we should admire in the man. It also occurs to me that these are traits Belinda Blumenthal admires and indeed has herself. Perhaps this is why she and Des do seem to retain their working relationship in this topsy turvey world of big business deals and international travel. But... we must never forget Des is the only Steele's employee who has actually worked for Bisch Herstellung and here is the story of his job interview...

Des Martin Blinked;
The job interviewer had just asked him to remove his jacket and shirt. Des smiled deeply to himself... he'd been waiting for this moment all his life. With a hint of a tease Des removed the offending garments, tossing them expertly onto an antique coat stand which was conveniently located in a corner of the interview room. The stand shook violently and gracefully fell over throwing the garments back at Des.

The job interviewer Blinked;

Des hastily got up from the white leather settee he was seated on and in the process knocked over his porcelain china cup of black coffee which he'd just been offered. The hot liquid splashed itself across the pristine white seat, burning its way into the delicate leather surface. Not knowing which way to turn, a flustered Des took a somewhat unwashed, grey handkerchief from deep down in his trouser pocket. He anxiously mopped the burning coffee off the leather leaving an unhealthy green slime in its place.

Unable to do anything better with the coffee sodden hanky Des turned his attention to the coat stand. He jumped up and grabbed the still vibrating, rustic metal antique, placing it back into its original corner. He skilfully smoothed down his rehung jacket and shirt, wiped the accumulating sweat from his forehead and dark hairy chest and returned to the settee. Des was no fool and placed his trouser clad ass over the green slime stain, hiding it temporarily from the job interviewer's incredulous view.

Des leant back, took a deep breath and said,
'Now where were we?'
The interviewer coughed and said,
'We veren't, I vas only getting started, but if you insist, vud you remove your shoes, socks and trousers?'
Des grinned and thought this was something he could do. Indeed, Des reckoned, he could become an expert at this sort of answer. He calmly stood up and kicked off his shiny black shoes, carefully directing them with some venom at the coat stand. He pulled off his socks and unzipped his trousers. With a meaningful flourish he pulled them down whilst keeping eye contact with the interviewer. Des skilfully threw them once again at the coat stand. This time the trousers caught a hook and the socks fell gracefully to the ground settling over his shoes. Now standing resplendent, legs apart in his skimpy black thong Des waited for the next question.

'My name is Valerie Bisch, Mr Martin and I vant to assure you that if you are successful in this job application you vill be reporting directly to me. As your UK Sales Director I vant you to know that I am only interested in vorking vith dedicated employees who vill go to the next step in clinching any sale. I repeat, going to the next step… do you vully understand?'

Des smiled and confidently replied,
'Yes Bitch… sorry Miss Bisch… Yish…. sorry, yes… I fully understand.'
'Do not call me Bitch again… Bitch…' as she glared at him.

Valerie put the paperwork she was holding in her delicately manicured
hands onto the desk and stood up. The extremely attractive brunette put
her hands behind her head and unloosed her hair. It majestically fell down
over her shoulders, giving Des a thrill of desire through his steadily rising
cock. Miss Bisch smiled inwardly to herself, noting the increasing area of
pale skin under the bulge in Des's skimpy thong. Valerie unbuttoned the
top button of her pristine white blouse. Des bulged further. Valerie
unfastened another button. Des bulged out of his thong…. free at last, his
cock blinked at its new surroundings.

Valerie Bisch ripped the last few buttons off her blouse, unable to control
herself any longer. They pinged and flew straight into Des Martin's eyes.
He yelped in pain and fell back onto the leather settee. Out of control,
Des's thong slipped down his slender frame, ending up around his legs,
effectively tripping him up. The imported East Berlin settee groaned, its
rear legs crumpled toppling Des onto the luxuriously carpeted floor. A
loudly yelping and blinded Des thrashed around trying to regain his
balance and composure. He needn't have bothered as Miss Bish had
everything under control.

Stepping around the fatally wounded white leather settee she placed her
six inch heel onto his foot. Des felt the cold steel make contact with his
writhing toes. His cock jumped in anticipation of greater things as Miss
Bisch stood over his splayed legs and arms and removed her remaining
garments. Naked except for her stilettos Valerie kicked Des's ass and
shouted,
'You vill shut up! Are you a man or ze mouse?'
Des' yelping decreased to one of whimpering, he'd never in all his wildest
dreams anticipated this scenario. He decided to let his cock do the talking
and shut up.

'Zere gut Mr Martin, ve vill make ze East Berliner of yu yet…. now, let's get
down to some real business.'
Miss Bisch lowered herself onto Des's rampant cock and started to
corkscrew her body into his. Des groaned in appreciation whilst Valerie
moaned in anticipation. Reasonably happy with her deep penetration of

Des's cock Valerie started to slowly stimulate her clitoris with her right hand's forefinger. Meanwhile Des had grabbed her ass with his two hands. His vision was now returning and he looked deeply into Valerie Bisch's eyes. He saw desire, ruthlessness and cruelty in the dirty yellow pool of fluorescent light lying behind her orange tinted contact lenses. Des gulped and helped her ass fuck him even harder.

After a short, but satisfactory period where Miss Bisch had orgasmed twice, she groggily stood up and went back to her desk. With East Berliner efficiency she gathered up the papers and tapped them into a neat bunch. She scrawled her signature across the top and addressed Des once again. 'Sit back on ze seat Herr Martin… or perhaps I call you, Sexy Dez…?'
Des smiled as he got to his knees and crawled to the destroyed white leather settee, dripping bodily fluids from Valerie's vagina and his own cock onto the expensively carpeted floor. He sat as best he could on the busted piece of furniture trying to look professional, if still naked.
Valerie continued, 'I like your resilience under ze pressure Sexy Dez, zo I'm going to offer you ze job. Eighty zousand of your Engleesh pounds, plus black East German Skoda car and perks… ze perks are only negotiable vith me zo vait for me in ze lobby and ve shall go for drinks, dinner and as you Engleesh call it, ze hanky panky, to celebrate your success…yez?'

Sexy Dez Blinked;

3. Isabella Candida "Donna" Ridley;

You either love Bella or you secretly love Bella. There are no other options. Her trademark voice was the first to emerge fully formed from Jamie's mouth during book two, and seems to have been the catalyst for the array of accents, dialects, and unusual utterances we've heard since. "An errant Jim Henson puppet", Alice once called her, and truer words were never spoken. A full-figured gal, and proud of it, Bella Ridley is a loyal friend and faithful bodyguard. She'll never not have her eye on your backside. What she lacks in brains, she sure makes up for in enthusiasm. When Bella's not sleeping her way to the top of the career ladder at literally incredible speed, she divides her time between;
Splurging on thoroughly unnecessary impulse purchases;
Performing Dickensian carol concerts;
Managing the fan club for an Australian TV chef;
Going bankrupt in Monopoly;
Drinking Chardonnay until she can barely speak (even less so than usual);
Miraculously recovering from comas;
Bingeing on McMassive Meal Deals with extra cheese string salsa;
Philosophising about testicles, and, of course;
Indulging in her favourite pastime: telly.

In other words, she's the prototypical millennial. There may be cloudy times ahead for Ms Ridley, given her best friend and mentor has just left Steele's for their biggest competitor, but I'm sure this will only add further layers to a personality already as complex as an all-day breakfast lasagne. Long may she live. (Just don't leave her in charge of the keycards.)

Rocky's Comment;
Donna, as I lovingly like to call Bella, after my monumental cock up at the very start of Book 1. Well, truth be told, I was testing you all out... and top marks to the team for catching me out.... and Jamie's story is true, we did discuss my "error" on the top of a double decker red London bus on our way to the Queens Tennis Club to watch a hopeful Andy Murray amongst others... what a great day out!! I did particularly well at the Moet et Chandon Tennis Tournament virtual game... and that was before I had any Chards...!

But back to Bella... and here's how she got onto the Glee Team... essentially, where it all started for her.

A fewish years ago;

'Bella.... stop yawning!'
Bella Candida Ridley sat upright. The warm June sun glinted through the classroom windows enticing her back to a gentle slumber with just the hint of a snore... that was her undoing.
She shook her head letting her long golden tresses fall around her shapely body, and tried to concentrate on the useless lesson she was currently attending as she'd just completed her last exams. It was no good, her heart wasn't in it, she needed to find a job with career prospects and get out of this dump. Besides, who could afford University these days with all those loans. Bella folded her arms on the desk and put her head down, she needed a 30 minute kip before she went back to her temporary night job at the Casino and now was the best opportunity she'd get all day.

The bell rang; Bella picked up her things and left school... forever; there was no way she was ever going back. Bella sauntered her way home, Mum and Dad lived... no existed, in an old pub in Bow, East London... some people thought it rough, but to Bella it was home. But what to do she thought, entering the sixth form at school had been an easy transition... it really sort of just happened... her grades were good, if not excellent so it was the obvious path. But that lazy warm day in mid June shouted out NOOOOOO, get a proper job, make the money, live your life...

'Miss B.C. Ridley!' the grey haired receptionist nodded at her across the foyer, pushing her bi-focals down her nose,
'Miss Sccchhhaaawwwwddddddeeer.. urgh.. de Klotz will see you now, just walk up one flight and go into the leather room on the right.'
Bella nodded, picked up her linen tote bag and went upstairs. This was exciting, an interview at Steele's Pots and Pans... whatever next?
A thinnish leggy blonde with tits to die for stuck her half shaven head out of an office doorway.
'Ridley??? Bella Candida??? with two d's...? Follow me!'
Bella Blinked;

Ssccc... de Klotz wagged her arse at Bella as she strutted down the corridor... Bella was intrigued. The sexy lady disappeared through a grey heavyish looking doorway, waving a finger for Bella to follow. She did, though to be honest it took a bit of strength to move the door. Perhaps it was a sophisticated health check up, with sensors attached to the door frame and hinges, measuring her internal mass, heart rate, cholesterol levels, body weight and athleticism all in one subtle second??? Bella was sure she'd pass... she hadn't been athletic sports champion three years in a row for nothing.

'Sit down.' de Klotz instructed...

'Feeling a bit hot?... well relax... just remove your jacket, whilst I get us some sparkling water.'

Bella relaxed onto the leather settee, thinking,

'I could get used to this sort of life....'

Bella Blinked;

Giselle Maarschalkerweerd de Klotz had just asked her to remove her blouse and skirt, Bella smiled in a quizzical sort of way but immediately did as she was requested. She was proud of her body and her matching skin tight bikini style briefs and brassiere showed it off at its best. Bella then started to slightly sweat as her bare skin encompassed the leather settee and the interviewer's questions became more personal.

'How many times a week do you have sex, Miss Ridley?'

'Are you comfortable with bi workmates, Miss Ridley?'

'How often do you wear a thong apart from weekends, Miss Ridley?'

Bella struggled through the questionable questions as best she could, and found that honesty was the best way to reply.

'Well... Miss Ridley,' the interviewer said at last, 'I'd like to offer you the job as receptionist. And if you accept I'd like to stage a roleplay regarding the possible extent of your duties here at Steele's Pots and Pans.'

Bella screamed in excitement, she'd done it, she'd gotten her first job; she was now on her way to becoming a captain of Industry, possibly even MD of Steele's Pots and Pans. The world was her oyster!

'Yes, yes and yes!' she screamed at Giselle jumping up and down in her semi undressed state.

'Good,' replied a smiling Giselle, 'now let's get on with your first roleplay... remove those undergarments!'

Bella Blinked;

Minutes later Giselle too was naked and started to handle Bella's tits, twisting her nipples as hard as she could. Bella groaned, this was way better than senior school. A shower with the other girls after soccer practice was a tame affair when compared with this blonde bombshell's skills. But Bella was a shrewd cookie and she hadn't grown up in East London without learning a few tricks of her own. While Giselle was destroying her tits, Bella's hands went to work on Giselle's clitoris. She started slowly vibrating it and gently applied more and more pressure until Giselle started to moan deeply... a couple of quick slaps saw Giselle squirt all over the fancy drinks cabinet standing to one side of the room. 'Oh dear,' Bella thought, 'just as well I'm not going for a cleaner's job.'

At that moment a tallish chap pushed his head around the closed office door.
'Ahem....' he interjected, 'I presume the interview went well Miss Maarschalkerweerd de Klotz?'
Giselle quickly came back to her senses and exclaimed,
'Tony... why yes, meet Bella Ridley our new receptionist as of today.'
Tony walked over and shook Bella's slippery hand.
He then gleefully licked it dry and said,
'Welcome aboard Bella, I'm Tony the MD, glad to see Giselle is getting your training started early!'
Bella blushed, and thought for the first time what was she getting herself into.
'Thank you, sir.' she replied.
'Please don't call me Sir, Bella,' Tony chuckled, 'leave that for our Chief Exec, Sir James Godwin. Oh by the way Giselle, he's called me to a meeting at the Pentra, join us when you've wrapped up this interview.'
Tony winked at Bella and left the room.
Bella Blinked;

It didn't take Giselle long to get back into her stride and this time she pushed Bella onto the leather settee, opened her long slender legs as wide as they'd go and greedily sucked her shaven vagina with gusto. Bella could only shriek in delight as Giselle continued to ravage her, happy in the knowledge that whatever this job didn't have, she would learn to love her bosses. Eventually Giselle had had her fill of Bella's juices and reversed the scenario. Bella was well and truly sated but found herself really up for the opportunity Giselle now presented her with. Her tongue flicked and licked Giselle's clitoris sending her into ecstasy. The shrieks of satisfaction spurred Bella on and by the end of her session she'd reduced Giselle to a sopping mess of sweat and vaginal liquids.

'Surely,' Bella thought, 'she was in no state to join a meeting with her M.D and Chief Exec in the next half hour?'

Giselle and Bella redressed casually discussing Bella's more mundane duties at Steele's Pots and Pans. She would start next week and after an induction period of two weeks the exiting receptionist would retire leaving Bella in charge.

'Wow,' Bella thought, 'how exciting, this surely beats the sixth form.'
Little did she then know the naivety of those words, but Bella Ridley was a fast learner and Giselle Maarschalkerweerd de Klotz a good teacher.

Three weeks later Bella arrived at work and sat down in her reception area, today was her first day in charge. A prime duty was to welcome members of staff by name as they walked through the foyer on their way to their offices.

'Morning Mr Thompson.'

'Morning Bella,' replied a beaming Jim... 'enjoy your first day in charge! Oh, I nearly forgot, here's a little present for you.'

Jim passed the small and nicely packaged package to Bella and went off whistling to his office.

Intrigued Bella quickly opened the wrapping and took out a petite black thong.

Bella Blinked;
...was Jim into her???

And she's really not stopped Blinking since, and no... Jim was under Belinda's orders... for the time being anyways.

Indeed, Bella Blinked so much she eventually took over the running of the sales team. Her love of the job quickly developed her addiction to English Sparkling Wine and the odd bottle of Champagne... never Cava and definitely not Prosecco. Her savvy pub owning parents were too smart to let her get attracted to the cheap stuff. And that showed when she joined Belinda on their Saturday morning trip to Forsters of Knightsbridge. The three or four complimentary bottles of Champagne which she necked back certainly oiled the purchase of her basic horse jumping kit. Indeed, I wonder if Forsters actually turned a profit on that sale. As always, her Boss Belinda, made them a handsome profit and show jumping was never really the same ever after. Pity.

So, there you have it, the first few days an innocent Bella Ridley was initiated into Steeles Pots and Pans. Not so many weeks later she was to meet her newest friend Belinda Blumenthal and that's now all history.

2. Gertrude, Duchess of Epsom;

Even in the pantheon of Flintstone creations, this mature lady with rags for breasts and a multipurpose riding crop is an unrivalled goddess. The Duchess is many things: overall head of British intelligence, goddaughter to the Queen, wife to the depraved Clarence, would-be champion skier, temporary leader of COCK, trainer to the most inspiring horse since Secretariat, and always... *always*... down for a good time. She's also got direct access to the launch buttons for the Trident nuclear missiles, which isn't at all concerning. Numbering Prime Ministers and bodybuilders among her lovers, the Duchess has somehow managed to keep a low profile despite driving around the English countryside with a horsebox and a Panama hat, exposing her own and her mistress' breasts to innocent service station attendants, and occasionally being left completely naked and delirious on the gravel drive of her country pile. (Whatever she's paying the household staff at Epsom Hall, it's not enough.) Her husky voice has become iconic, as have her three-inch nipples. And her mysterious past... remember Swiss skiing instructor François Gerard and the reveal that she has a lost child by him?... is one of those dangling threads which Rocky leaves so tantalisingly open to possibility. The Duchess' steady hand will be needed more than ever in light of Belinda's shocking decision to leave the company. We haven't heard the last of "Dirty Gertie".

Rocky's Comment;
This lady... because she's too old to be called a girl, is someone who should be a girl in the Belinda Blinked franchise. If I had to ever rewrite the books... say for a movie, I would recast Gertrude as a sassy 39 year old. At the top of her game... whatever that might be... but I'd still keep those riveting nipples and breasts... well, I would change one itsy bitsy detail... her breast shape... Yes, I'd revamp her bust size to one that would equal Belinda's and Bella's and why not go the whole hog and include the slimmer Giselle who's tits notoriously fell down like "pomegranates" in the Pentra bar. Yes, in a remodelling of the original characters the Duchess would be 20+ years younger and a much more accomplished horsebox trailer driver. But that's enough of my indulgences... here's the story where the Duchess books herself into a Breast Remodelling Clinic and attains those attributes, I've just been discussing...

It was hot, passenger Gertrude Bromley mopped her brow for the second time in ten minutes. She listened attentively to the garbled tannoy messages shouted out at random in Guarulhos Airport. There was one particular flight she was waiting for, the 1.47pm to Manaus, North Brazil. Her previous twelve-hour flight from London Heathrow was comfortable; Business VClass did at least guarantee a restful 10 hour sleep... but the next flight didn't do Business... of any sort. It was going to be a ball breaker and the Duchess knew what that meant. She'd always acknowledged that travelling incognito on her own special mission (which was so important to her deflated self-esteem) meant that her final destination was unknown... well, to everyone except Surgeon Marco Ouriques. Yes, Gertrude was at last going to do something about those paper-thin tits and of course Belinda's pal, Jim Stirling had highly recommended her horse racing acquaintance Marco... what was a lady to do?

At last, the boarding gate was announced... just 12 minutes before the gate closed... Gertrude moaned, she'd been warned about the last minuteness of Brazil, but this was ridiculous... 12 minutes to walk the length of an international airport... it was lunacy but, hey TIB, This Is Brazil. At that moment a suave young gentleman gripped her elbow... 'Madame, have no worries, I am not from the Red Flag brigade to kidnap you, instead I am a highly qualified Red Cap and I shall whisk you on my electric trolley to your boarding gate...' Under his breath he added... 'Senior Ouriques has reserved it.'
Gertrude gasped as only a middle aged lady could and tumbled into his arms whilst ensuring she kept hold of her dark leather satchel.
'Alas Madame, we have no time for ze hanky panky... we must get there in ten minutes or we are lost...'
With that he gunned his electric motor and the silicon moulded tyres gripped the marble floor with a swoosh. In five minutes Gertrude found herself buckled into her flight seat with her hand luggage safely stowed. Seconds later the aircraft taxied and took off. Gertrude Bromley fell deeply asleep.

Three hours and forty-eight minutes later Gertrude walked down the steps of her Sao Paulo plane into a hell hole of humidity.
'God,' she thought, 'I don't need an orgasm to get wet here... I'm totally wet all over.'

She smiled and thought again...
'But I like it...'
The head of the MI6 British secret service walked across the rain soaked tarmac and collected her luggage. Another hand gripped her elbow...
'Come with me Madame, Sr. Ouriques has transport waiting for you.'
Gertrude gasped longingly at the stunningly physical masculinity of her new companion... and he knew he would have her completely in the back of his mini-van. It was what he did to those who wanted that little extra attention in his home city... after all, he like God, was Brazilian and like God, he didn't charge for the extra services... he just needed a good tip.... which he always earned...

A much dishevelled Duchess arrived slightly behind schedule at her hotel opposite the world famous Manaus Opera House. Her delicious driver checked her in, took her to her room, stripped her of her clothing and put her in the shower. Duty done he left her to her soap and towels. The 50$US tip cheered him wonderfully. If Ouriques was as loyal as he'd always been, he'd be first in line to drive this one back to the airport and he'd make sure to sample the new attributes... whatever they were.

A good night's sleep with a medium rare room service and pomme frites steak somewhere in the middle, saw Gertrude up and running the next morning, albeit 6.00am Manaus time. An early morning telephone call from Surgeon Ouriques confirmed breakfast with his latest patient. By midday they were travelling up river to his Clinic in the heart of the Amazon. Gertrude was getting nervous as the reality of what she'd signed up to hit her. Sat in the rear of the powerful racing motor boat she stroked her wafer thin tits for what was probably the last time, but deep down she had no regrets. She gently fondled the leather suitcase she'd dutifully carried from the tech department of MI6 back in central London. Soon it's liquid contents would be placed inside her tits and she would once again become undeniable to male or female. Now even in the humid river heat she started to shiver from excitement. The boat pulled into a small jetty, she'd arrived... it was now or... never?

Marco sat down opposite Gertrude and handed her a small glass of Chardonnay wine.
'You know Duchess...'

'Stop... Marco, call me Gertie... it's important to me not only from a security point of view, but also to me in a moving on sort of way from my old paper thin tits... do you understand?'

She looked pleadingly at him. He smiled, nodded his head and said,

'Good... this is a very positive route to take Gertrude... Gertie, and be assured I always test drive my work, you will not leave disappointed in any way.'

Once again, his golden smile spread across his face and Gertrude felt a frisson of excitement waft through her vagina.

'Besides,' he added,

'Belinda would kill me if I failed you.'

Gertrude laughed and added,

'OK, I'm ready... here's my leather satchel with my very sophisticated implant silicon... do it.'

Ouriques opened the satchel and whistled...

'Wow Duchess... if I put all this lot in, you'd never fit through a restaurant door again....'

Gertie Blinked;

1. Belinda Bounty Blumenthal;

It would have been a disgrace not to place the Queen of découpage and the champion kisser of the Kentish Board Games Society at number one. With sales experience across multiple continents, Belinda Blumenthal is...
always prepared (that briefcase never leaves her side),
eternally punctual (her calendar is imprinted on her mind at all times),
unapologetic (especially about her sexy black thong),
intuitive (gifted with the unusual olfactory ability to tell your past based on what your socks smell like),
inspiring (rousing speeches or choral chants can be provided at a moment's notice),
and a talented manager of employees (she uses a reward-based approach for her direct staff).
But just don't crash your bloody car, okay?

Guided by her undying faith in the Norse Gods, she will always make you feel comfortable and safe when getting down to business, whether 15,000 feet in the sky or in a dingy basement flat. And no matter whether she finds herself in a medium-sized garden maze or a hot air balloon above the dust and scrub, Belinda navigates the situation with all the expertise of Jamie Morton backstage at the Club Theatre. It helps that she has some kind of family fortune (that Thai mahogany tile floor won't pay for itself) and the ability to go without sleep or bathing for weeks at a time.

Her only weakness, and it's a big one, is an insatiable need for turkey. Belinda didn't express herself much in book one, to the chagrin of Alice, James, and millions of others, but she's exploded in an array of colours since then, including demonstrating remarkable adroitness with a travel spanner. She's provided us with so many mantras and axioms over the years. My personal favourite must be "harness the ordinary person and you can rule the world" which, disgracefully, hasn't yet been included in the Oxford Dictionary of Quotations.

Ultimately, Belinda is a role model for all young people around the world, reminding us that it may be hard work but we *can* have it all:
Turkey;
Chardonnay;
Friends;

Fortune;

And red chilli sex;

Now that she's President and Chief Operating Executive Officer (you know, PCOEO) of Bisch Herstellung Enterprises, things are taking an unexpected new direction for our bad bitch of business. And I, for one, can't wait.

Rocky's Comment;

Belinda Blinked;

It wasn't a dream...

Or was it...

She turned over and fell back into a fitful sleep.

Belinda started to snore...

Her husband Des nudged her gently.

'Fuck off Des, I need my sleep, I've got one hell of a day tomorrow and you know it. Once again, I've got to go to court to get you off another fucking parking fine... fuck off!'

Des smirked in the darkness of their one bedroom crummy rented council flat on the outskirts of central London. But he acknowledged she was right. His fluorescent orange town car taxi business had gotten him into deeper parking fines than he could pay and of course Belinda would bale him out. Not that she earned much, a jodhpur sales girl in Forsters of Knightsbridge would never be a top earner, especially as the Boss, Cedric Forster, kept deducting monies from her pay packet for "indecent exposure to clients" whatever that meant. Well, if you sell fucking jodhpurs you're going to show some ass in the sales demos...??

Des caressed Belinda's tits and drifted back to sleep.

'Well, that didn't go too bad Belinda,' Des chuckled as they left court....

'and that old trout of a Justice of the Peace hired me to take her bridge club out on the town next Saturday night... ching ching!!'

'Fuck off Des... drop me off at work, I've got a big American client calling in today for a special fitting. Cedric says if I fuck it up, I'm fired...'

'Belinda... my darling... with tits like yours and an ass to die for, there's no way you won't get the sale.' Des winked at her and pulled out into the traffic.

'Delighted to meet you Mr Stirling... and your companion...?

'Gee Belinder, it's great to be in your hands… I was worried that old clown… whaddya call him… Search… no no… I got it, Cedric, would be fitting me… I just don't like male hands near my special bits so to speak…. Sorry, forgot my manners… this here beautiful lady is Bella… Bella Ridley… you've probably seen her on British TV… yeah… she's main anchor at CCB studios programme NewsDays. But enough of us… where's the gear… oh could you get Bella a glass of Champagne???'
Belinda replied slightly pompously,
'Oh I'm so sorry Mr Stirling, we're all out of Champagne… would English Sparkling Wine do… Denbies??? Chapeldown… Simpsons from Canterbury???
'No worries Belinder… if it's bubbly, Bella will drink it…!'
He smiled at Bella who sat down on the white leather recliner and held out her hands and breathed….
'Doubles please.'

Belinda went to the overly ornate mahogany drinks cabinet situated in the corner of the display area and poured three not two, glasses of England's finest bubbly. Please join your companion, Mr Stirling, on the recliner whilst I play you our introductory video… it will answer all the questions you've been asking yourself about the British and International Equestrian scene in the space of only five minutes… and then… I'm all yours…'
Bella Belched;

Belinda pressed the buttons on the digital device and retired behind a discreet curtain. The room went dark and the intro music played.

Five minutes later Belinda pulled the curtain aside, dressed only in a stunning set of off white/khaki jodhpurs. Her glamorous tits were hung like pomegranates and Jim smiled.
'Gee Belinder… I just love pickin low hanging fruit… ask Bella here…'
Jim guffawed and finished off the bottle Belinda had unobtrusively set down between them before she played the demo.
'Why Mr Stirling… sir… I'd expect nothing else…'
Belinda smiled as she walked up and down in her skin tight attire letting her breasts swell and sway as her nipples hardened in front of the very big money.
Bella Belched again and Belinda took a second bottle from the drinks cabinet.

'Having seen the jodphurs, would Sir like to view the mole skin jackets??'
'Why yes Belinder... as long as they're not too tight fitting around the breasts?
Jim smiled and nodded a nod to Belinda as if saying....
'Just you keep those titties on view and we'll be right dandy!'
And Belinda did just that... having disappeared behind the curtain for the second time she re-emerged with a beautiful red coat and black trimmings. Leaving the silver buttons on the front unbuttoned she swaggered into the fitting room with her breasts swinging wildly like Tarzan amongst the jungle tree trunks.
Bella immediately put down her half finished glass and stood up.
'Jim,' she declared, 'I want that coat and I want it now!'
Jim mouthed a big 'Yes' and stripped it off Belinda. Bella immediately removed all her upper garments revealing her very own measly thin tits and miniscule nipples. The coat enveloped her in red moleskin much to the chagrin of her companion.

'Anything smaller Belinder?' he cried out.
'Why yes sir... follow me to the stock room.'
Belinda took off and a sweating Jim followed her up the old staircase. At the top Belinda removed her tight jodhpurs and now completely bare advanced on Jim.
'Come here my man and I'll give you a roasting spit of a good time.'
In five seconds flat Belinda had stripped Jim back to his boxer shorts and smothered him in the sexual liquids emanating from all her dripping orifices. Jim was stunned, but never to be backward pulled off his waist covering and let his massive todger enter the fray.
'Wowwww,' Belinda gasped,
'that is one hell of a dick Jim... and what a magnificent specimen it surely is.'
Jim smiled and contemptuously stuffed it up Belinda's ass.
'I hope ya likes em big Belinder... cause that's all we do in Texas!'
Belinda Blinked;
Somewhere in the far distance...
Bella Belched;

Thank you, Sammy, for putting Belinda first in this mish mash of Blinking character ratings. I too feel she completely deserves to be there, at the top, leading the way for all modern business women. Do you remember one of her favourite mantras...

"When you get what you want... you feel great!'

I love to write this one when I'm signing an original book for a fan, it just epitomises her character so succinctly. Belinda Blumenthal will always be my favourite character in the series, because quite simply there would be no books without her. The "Belinda Blinked" endings to the odd paragraph and at the end of many chapters is another way in which she has become a percussive writing tool which many authors are now imitating... and good for them. I love to use alliterations and with the BBB storyline it was fascinating just how many BBB's I was able to introduce into the script. Benny Bella's Brother being one such example.

I'm glad Sammy alluded to Belinda having some sort of fortune stacked behind her and I hope you're considering where it may have come from. All I can say is that, this will be resolved in the near future as I release a couple of books which will bring you further into the Belinda Blumenthal world of big business and sexy romps...

The Conclusion;

We are now at the end of our monumental journey through the Belinda Blinked Character Rankings and it only remains for me to say thank you to Sammy and all you Belinkers who will have now widened your already immaculate knowledge of the series, immensely. But wait... you do know there's more to come... so until next time I wish you all a happy and fulfilling life and remember...
life is shit...
but we all move on...

Rocky Blinked;

Our websites where you can find extra content or breaking events...

www.mydadwroteaporno.com

www.BelindaBlinked.com

www.RockyFlintstone.com

and why not visit Rocky's merchandise store.

Just search RockysPavilion on Etsy!!

Back to contents…

Printed in Great Britain
by Amazon

31556292R00101